DIEU ET MON DROIT

THE SUNDAY TIMES

Brain Teasers

Book 1

200 mind-boggling riddles

Published in 2019 by Times Books

HarperCollins*Publishers*
Westerhill Road
Bishopbriggs
Glasgow, G64 2QT

www.collinsdictionary.com

10 9 8 7 6 5 4 3 2 1

ISBN 978-0-00-834372-9

Typeset by Davidson Publishing Solutions, Glasgow

Printed and bound by CPI Group (UK) Ltd, Croydon CR0 4YY

A catalogue record for this book is available from the British Library.

If you would like to comment on any aspect of this book, please contact us at the above address or online via email: puzzles@harpercollins.co.uk

Follow us on Twitter @collinsdict
Facebook.com/CollinsDictionary

CONTENTS

INTRODUCTION

Welcome to this new collection of Brain Teasers. Here we bring together 200 mind-bending puzzles from the series, which appears every week in *The Sunday Times* under the shortened name of Teaser. This is the first collection since 2002, and I am delighted that these ingenious challenges are enjoying a fresh outing in book form.

Each Brain Teaser takes the form of a paragraph or two of text, sometimes accompanied by a diagram. The puzzles invariably require the application of mathematical or logical reasoning to reach the answer, and, like any true intellectual challenge, completing one offers great satisfaction to the solver.

The Brain Teasers in this book were originally published between November 2014, and September 2018. This period spans the editorships of two brilliant colleagues who, between them, have overseen the publication of each Brain Teaser that appears in these pages. Dr Victor Bryant edited the puzzle for more than 40 years before handing the baton to John Owen at the end of 2017. I am immensely grateful to Victor and John for all their efforts in making the series such a success over their years at the helm.

Both editors also contribute puzzles to the series, complementing those submitted by many other regular and occasional setters. The seemingly endless ingenuity of our setters is nothing short of astonishing, and I would like to thank them all for the entertainment they continue to provide. The setter of each puzzle in this book is given at the back.

All Brain Teaser submissions are unsolicited and anyone with a good idea is welcome to send in a puzzle. If you have been inspired by the puzzles in this book and would like to write a Brain Teaser puzzle for publication in *The Sunday Times*, please email: puzzles.feedback@sunday-times.co.uk for more information.

David Parfitt
Puzzles Editor, *The Times & The Sunday Times*

BRAIN TEASERS

1 | FOURSUMS

In a woodwork lesson the class was given a list of four different non-zero digits. Each student's task was to construct a rectangular sheet whose sides were two-figure numbers of centimetres with the two lengths, between them, using the four given digits. Pat constructed the smallest possible such rectangle and his friend constructed the largest possible. The areas of these two rectangles differed by half a square metre.

What were the four digits?

2 | BETTER TETRA

I have four tetrahedra that I use as dice: each has four identical triangular faces and on each face of each dice is one of the numbers 1, 2, 3 or 4 (repeats being allowed). No dice uses the same four numbers and, for each dice, the sum of its four numbers is ten. I play a game with my friend. We each throw a dice and choose the face-down number: sometimes it's a draw, otherwise the higher number wins. I am always more likely to win. So my friend changes the rules. We now throw our dice twice, add the two numbers, and the higher total wins. Now he knows that there is one dice he can choose that will win more often than the others.

What are the four numbers on that winning dice?

3 | MILLINER'S HAT-TRICK

A football tournament has four groups of four teams, with the teams in the same group playing each other once. So far the teams have played two games and in each group the distribution of points is different. Also, in each group just one pair of teams are level on points and their positions have been determined by their "goals scored". Milliner has scored four (including a hat-trick), Orlando two, and nine other players have scored one goal each. Despite his success, Orlando's team is not the top of its group.

What are the results of the two games that Milliner's team has played and the two games that Orlando's team has played?

4 | A SIMPLE SUM

I have written down two three-figure numbers and one four-figure number: between them they use each of the digits 0 to 9 exactly once. In fact the four-figure number is the sum of the other two numbers.

If I told you how many of the three numbers were even, then it would be possible to work out the four-figure number.

What is it?

5 | ST ANDREW'S DAY

Bearing in mind today's date, I have written down two numbers in code, with different letters being used consistently to replace different digits. The addition of the two numbers is shown below, appropriately leading to today's date as a six-figure number.

	S	A	I	N	T
A	N	D	R	E	W
3	0	1	1	1	4

What is the number to SEND?

6 | HEADCOUNT

My grandson and I play a coin game. First we toss seven coins and I have to predict in advance the number of heads whilst he has to predict the number of tails. I then get a number of points equal to the number of heads, he gets a number of points equal to the number of tails, and anyone whose prediction was correct gets a fixed bonus number of points (less than 40). We repeat this with six coins in the second round, then five, and so on down to two. In a recent game we noticed that, after each round, the total of all the points so far awarded was equal to a prime number.

What is the "fixed bonus" number of points, and what was the total of all the points at the end of the game?

7 | CHRISTMAS STAR

I asked Peter to place the numbers 1 to 10 at the ten intersection points of the Christmas star so that in each of the five lines the four numbers added to the same total. He found that this was impossible so instead he did it with the numbers 1 to 9 together with just one of those digits repeated. In his answer there was just one line in which that digit did not appear.

What were the four numbers in that line?

8 | GARDEN DESIGN

I have a square garden with sides a whole number of metres in length. It is surrounded by a fence with posts at the corners and then at one metre intervals. I wish to make the garden into four triangular beds surrounding a lawn that has four sides of different lengths. To mark out the lawn I choose one post on each of the sides of the garden and I stretch a length of string around those four posts. I can create my lawn in various ways but the length of string needed is always one of two possible values. I have chosen one arrangement using the smaller of the two lengths.

What is the area of my lawn?

9 | FACTORIAL FACT

The "factorials" of numbers are defined by 1! = 1, 2! = 2x1, 3! = 3x2x1, 4! = 4x3x2x1, etc.

It is possible to take eleven of the twelve factorials 1!, 2!, 3!, 4!, 5!, 6!, 7!, 8!, 9!, 10!, 11!, 12! and to split them into groups of three, four and four so that in each group the product of the factorials in that group is a perfect square.

What are the factorials in the group whose product is the smallest?

10 | IT'S A LOTTERY

I regularly entered the Lottery, choosing six numbers from 1 to 49. Often some of the numbers drawn were mine but with their digits in reverse order. So I now make two entries: the first entry consists of six two-figure numbers with no zeros involved, and the second entry consists of six entirely different numbers formed by reversing the numbers in the first entry. Interestingly, the sum of the six numbers in each entry is the same, and each entry contains just two consecutive numbers.

What (in increasing order) are the six numbers in the entry that contains the highest number?

11 | CITY SNARL-UP

I had to drive the six miles from my home into the city centre. The first mile was completed at a steady whole number of miles per hour (and not exceeding the 20mph speed limit). Then each succeeding mile was completed at a lower steady speed than the previous mile, again at a whole number of miles per hour.

After two miles of the journey my average speed had been a whole number of miles per hour, and indeed the same was true after three miles, after four miles, after five miles, and at the end of my journey.

How long did the journey take?

12 | PRIME MEAT

Mark has recently converted from vegetarianism. John sent him a coded message consisting of a list of prime numbers. Mark found that by systematically replacing each digit by a letter the list became the message:

EAT BEEF AT TIMES

IT IS A PRIME MEAT

What number became PRIME?

13 | LETTER-WRITING

Last year I went to calligraphy lessons. They were held weekly, on the same day each week, for nine consecutive months. Actually I only went to 15 of the lessons, and after the course was over I listed the dates of those lessons that I had attended. In order to practise my new skills I wrote the dates in words (in the format "First of January" etc) and I found to my surprise that each date used a different number of letters.

What were the dates of the first and last lessons that I attended?

14 | INTERLOCKING SQUARES

Place all of the digits 0 to 9 in the grid so that, reading across or down in crossword fashion, one can see a two-figure square, a three-figure square, and two four-figure squares.

What (in increasing order) are the four squares?

15 | TWO TO CHOOSE

I told Sue a two-figure number and I told Terry another two-figure number, one of which was a multiple of the other. I explained this to them but knew that neither of them would be able to work out the other number. (In fact, if they had to guess the other number Sue had three times as many choices as Terry – but I did not tell them that.) When Sue confirmed that it was impossible for her to work out Terry's number, he was then able to work out her number.

What were their numbers?

16 | HS2

Last night I dreamt that I made a train journey on the HS2 line. The journey was a whole number of miles in length and it took less than an hour. From the starting station the train accelerated steadily to its maximum speed of 220mph, then it continued at that speed for a while, and finally it decelerated steadily to the finishing station. If you took the number of minutes that the train was travelling at a steady speed and reversed the order of its two digits, then you got the number of minutes for the whole journey.

How many miles long was the journey?

17 | PRIME DAY FOR THE IRISH

St Patrick's Day is March 17 and it is a prime day in many ways: What number month? 3; What number day? 17; How many letters in "March"? 5; How many days in March? 31.

I asked Pat the same questions about his birthday this year – but I simply asked whether the four answers were prime or not. When he had told me he said "now, if I told you its day of the week this year, you should be able to work out my birthday." Then, without me actually being told the day, I was indeed able to work out his birthday.

What is his birthday?

18 | FUNNY DICE

I have two cube-shaped dice, one red and one blue, with a positive whole number on each face. When I throw the dice and add up the two numbers, the most likely total is 7. The next most likely totals are 6 and 8, the next are 5 and 9, the next are 4 and 10, the next are 3 and 11, and the least likely are 2 and 12. However, my dice are not standard: indeed, the total of the six numbers on the red dice is higher than the total of those on the blue dice.

What are the six numbers on the red dice?

19 | X TIMES

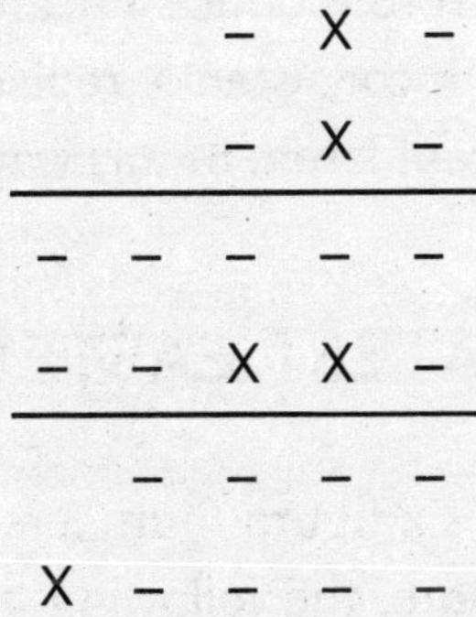

In this long multiplication sum, I am multiplying a three-figure number by itself. Throughout the workings one particular digit has been replaced by X wherever it occurs. All other digits have been replaced by a dash.

What is the three-figure number being squared?

20 | NEATER EASTER TEASER

In my latest effort to produce a neater Easter Teaser I have once again consistently replaced each of the digits by a different letter. In this way

NEATER LATEST EASTER TEASER

represent four six-figure numbers in increasing order. Furthermore, the following addition sum is correct:

```
 F L O R A L
 E A S T E R
 -----------
 B O N N E T
```

What is the BONNET's value?

21 | HYMNS BORED

Peter became bored during the Sunday service, so his mind turned to the three three-figure hymn numbers displayed on the board, all chosen from the five hundred hymns in the hymnal. He noticed that the sum of the digits for each hymn was the same, that one hymn number was the average of the other two, and that no digit appeared more than once on the board.

What (in increasing order) were the three hymn numbers?

22 | LINE-UP

I have arranged the numbers from 1 to 27 in a three-by-three-by-three cubical array. I have noticed that the nine numbers making up one of the faces of the cube are all primes. Also, I have searched through the array and written down the sum of any three numbers that are in a straight line. I have then calculated the grand total of all those line-sums. It turns out that the grand total is itself a perfect cube!

What is that grand total?

23 | THE SCHOOL RUN

Each of the three houses of Merryhouse School entered four students in the cross-country race. Points were awarded with 12 for the winner, 11 for second, and so on down to 1 for the tail-ender (from Berry House). When the points were added up, all houses had equal points. Three of the runners from Cherry House were in consecutive positions, as were just the two middle-performers from Derry House.

Which house did the winner come from, and what were the individual scores of its runners?

24 | SQUARE CUT

Jorkens, the wily old cricketer, is faced with a new type of square cut. His house has three square bedrooms, all of different sizes. He has just bought a new carpet for the largest bedroom and has cut up its old carpet into four rectangular pieces, the smallest of which has an area of four square metres. He is able to use the four pieces to carpet the other two bedrooms exactly.

What is the area of the largest bedroom?

25 | MARBLE JAR

At our local fete one of the games consisted of guessing the number of marbles in a jar: some of the marbles were red and the rest were blue. People had to guess how many there were of each colour. The organiser gave me a couple of clues. Firstly, he told me that there were nearly four hundred marbles altogether. Secondly, he told me that if, when blindfolded, I removed four marbles from the jar, then the chance that they would all be red was exactly one in a four-figure number.

How many red marbles were there, and how many blue?

26 | DARTS MATCH

Andrew, Alexander, Austin, Anthony, Benjamin, Charles, Christopher, Elijah, Jacob, Jayden, Jackson, James, Jason, Mason, Michael, Nathan, Newman, Robert, Samuel and William entered a darts competition, arranged into five teams of four players. It turned out that, for any pair of members of any team, there were just two letters of the alphabet that occurred (once or more) in both their names. The names in each team were arranged alphabetically, the first name being the captain and the last name the reserve. Then the teams were numbered 1 to 5 in alphabetical order of the captains.

In the order 1 to 5, who were the reserves?

27 | ROUND THE RIVER

My school holds "Round the river" runs – a whole number of metres to a bridge on the river and then the same number of metres back. Some years ago I took part with my friends Roy, Al, David and Cy. We each did the outward half at our own steady speeds (each being a whole number of centimetres per minute). For the return half I continued at my steady speed, Roy increased his speed by 10%, Al increased his speed by 20%, David increased his by 30%, and Cy increased his by 40%. We all finished together in a whole number of minutes, a little less than half an hour.

What (in metres) is the total length of the race?

28 | GRANNY'S BIRTHDAYS

At Granny's birthday this year she was telling us some surprising things about some past birthdays. She told us that each year she writes down the date of her birthday (in the eight-digit form dd/mm/yyyy) and her age in years. On two occasions in her lifetime it has turned out that this has involved writing each of the digits 0 to 9 exactly once. The first of these occasions was in 1974.

What is Granny's date of birth (in the eight-digit form)?

29 | RED-HANDED

I removed an even number of red cards from a standard pack and I then divided the remaining cards into two piles. I drew a card at random from the first pile and it was black (there was a whole-numbered percentage chance of this happening). I then placed that black card in the second pile, shuffled them, and chose a card at random from that pile. It was red (and the percentage chance of this happening was exactly the same as that earlier percentage).

How many red cards had I removed from the pack?

30 | BEST BEFORE

Peter likes to note "pandigital" times, such as 15:46, 29/03/78, that use all ten digits. Here the five individual numbers (15, 46, 29, 3 and 78) have a product that is divisible by the perfect square 36, and they also have a sum that is two more than a perfect square. He has been watching for pandigital times ever since and remembers one where the product of the five numbers was not divisible by any perfect square (apart from 1!): this has never happened since! He is also looking out for a pandigital time where the sum of the five numbers is a perfect square.

(a) When was that last "non-square" pandigital time?

(b) When will that first "square-sum" pandigital time be?

31 | NO QUESTION ABOUT IT!

"Sign Works" make rectangular signs of all sizes. Pat ordered a sign for the pub with the following instructions. "The length must be twice the width. Furthermore, the dimensions should be such that if you take its length (in centimetres), square the sum of its digits and take away the length itself, then you get the width. On the other hand, if you take its width (in centimetres), square the sum of its digits and take away the width itself, then you get the length." This was enough information for the signmaker to calculate the dimensions of the sign.

What were they?

32 | FAMILY HISTORY

Three of George's relatives who were born in different years of the 20th century shared the same birthday. Writing these in the form D/M/Y with just two digits for the year, he tells Martha that: in one case D divided by M, when expressed as a percentage, is Y; in another M is the average of D and Y; in the remaining one D raised to the power M equals Y. George then told Martha that knowing the day, D, would not enable her to work out the three dates, but knowing any one of the three years would enable her to work out all three dates.

What is the most recent of the three birth dates?

33 | FEMALE DOMINATION

In the village of Alphaville, the number of females divided by the number of males was a certain whole number. Then one man and his wife moved into the village and the result was that the number of females divided by the number of males was one less than before. Now today two more such married couples have moved into the village, but the number of females divided by the number of males is still a whole number.

What is the population of the village now?

34 | TERRIBLE TEENS

I have allocated a numerical value (possibly negative) to each letter of the alphabet, where some different letters may have the same value. I can now work out the value of any word by adding up the values of its individual letters. In this way NONE has value 0, ONE has value 1, TWO has value 2, and so on up to ELEVEN having value 11. Unfortunately, looking at the words for the numbers TWELVE to NINETEEN, I find that only two have values equal to the number itself.

Which two?

35 | SPORTS QUIZ

A sports quiz featured one footballer, one cricketer and one rugby player each week. Over the six-week series the footballers featured were (in order) Gerrard, Lambert, Lampard, Rooney, Smalling and Welbeck. The cricketers were (in some order) Carberry, Compton, Robson, Shahzad, Stokes and Tredwell. The rugby players (in some order) were Cipriani, Launchbury, Parling, Robshaw, Trinder and Twelvetrees. Each week, for any two of the three names, there were just two different letters of the alphabet that occurred in both names (with the letters possibly occurring more than once).

List the cricketers in the order in which they appeared.

36 | SQUARE DANCE

Dancers numbered from 1 to 9 were about to perform a square dance: five were dressed in red and the rest in blue. They stood in a three-by-three array with all three dancers in the first row wearing red and all three in another row wearing blue. Their numbers formed a magic square (ie, the sum of the three numbers in any row, column or diagonal was the same). One of the dancers in red looked around and noted that the sum of the numbers of the four other dancers in red was the same as the sum of the numbers of the four dancers in blue. One of the dancers in blue was number 8.

What were the numbers of the other three dancers in blue?

37 | KING LEAR II

King Lear II had a square kingdom divided into 16 equal smaller squares. He kept one square and divided the rest equally among his daughters, giving each one an identically-shaped connected piece. If you knew whether Lear kept a corner square, an edge square or a middle square, then you could work out how many daughters he had. The squares were numbered 1 to 16 in the usual way. The numbers of Cordelia's squares added up to a perfect square. If you now knew that total you could work out the number of Lear's square.

What number square did Lear keep for himself and what were the numbers of Cordelia's squares?

38 | PRIME LOCATION

I have a rectangular garden with an area of just over one hectare. It is divided exactly into three parts – a lawn, a flower bed and a vegetable patch. Each of these three areas is a right-angled triangle with sides a whole number of metres in length. A fence runs along two adjacent sides of the rectangular garden. The length of the fence is a prime number of metres.

What are the dimensions of the rectangular garden?

39 | DIGITAL SHUFFLE

George and Martha have nine cards with a different non-zero digit on each. To teach their nephew to count they lined up the cards in increasing order. He then rearranged the order of the line and Martha was impressed when she noticed that no digit was in its original position. George was even more impressed when he found that the six-figure number formed by the last six cards was the square of the three-figure number formed by the first three.

What was that three-figure number?

40 | WHAT A GEM!

A friend showed me a beautiful gem with shiny flat faces and lots of planes of symmetry. After a quick examination I was able to declare that it was "perfectly square". This puzzled my friend because none of the faces had four edges. So I explained by pointing out that the gem's number of faces was a perfect square, its number of edges was a perfect square, and its number of vertices was a perfect square.

How many faces did it have, and how many of those were triangular?

41 | GOLF CHALLENGE

Mark and John played 18 holes of golf: the holes consisting of six each of par 3, par 4 and par 5. Each player finished the round in 72, consisting of six 3s, six 4s and six 5s. In fact each of them had six birdies (one under par), six on par, and six bogies (one over par). At no hole did the two players take the same number of strokes, and Mark beat John on ten of the holes.

How many of Mark's winning holes were
(a) on par 3 holes?
(b) on par 4 holes?
(c) on par 5 holes?

42 | THREE LITTLE LISTS

I have chosen five different numbers, each less than 20, and I have listed these numbers in three ways. In the first list the numbers are in increasing numerical order. In the second list the numbers are written in words and are in alphabetical order. In the third list they are again in words and as you work down the list each word uses more letters than its predecessor. Each number is in a different position in each of the lists.

What are my five numbers?

43 | PRIME POINTS

In my fantasy football league each team plays each other once, with three points for a win and one point for a draw. Last season Aberdeen won the league, Brechin finished second, Cowdenbeath third, and so on, in alphabetical order. Remarkably each team finished with a different prime number of points. Dunfermline lost to Forfar.

In order, what were Elgin's results against Aberdeen, Brechin, Cowdenbeath, and so on (in the form WWLDL...)?

44 | TWO BY TWO

Animals board the ark in pairs:

EWE and RAM
HEN and COCK

In fact these are numbers with letters consistently replacing digits; one pair of the numbers being odd, the other pair being even, and both pairs have the same sum. The three digits of the number ARK are consecutive digits in a muddled order. All this information uniquely determines the number NOAH.

What is the number NOAH?

45 | CUTTING CORNERS

To make an unusual paperweight a craftsman started with a cuboidal block of marble whose sides were whole numbers of centimetres, the smallest sides being 5cm and 10cm long. From this block he cut off a corner to create a triangular face; in fact each side of this triangle was the diagonal of a face of the original block. The area of the triangle was a whole number of square centimetres.

What was the length of the longest side of the original block?

46 | IN THE BAG

A set of snooker balls consists of fifteen reds and seven others. From my set I put some into a bag. I calculated that if I picked three balls out of the bag simultaneously at random, then there was a one in a whole-number chance that they would all be red. It was more likely that none of the three would be red – in fact there was also a one in a whole-number chance of this happening.

How many balls did I put in the bag, and how many of those were red?

47 | COMING HOME

George, Martha and their daughter all drive at their own steady speeds (whole numbers of mph), the daughter's speed being 10mph more than Martha's. One day George left home to drive to his daughter's house at the same time as she left her house to visit her parents: they passed each other at the Crossed Keys pub. Another time Martha left her daughter's to return home at the same time as her daughter started the reverse journey: they too passed at the Crossed Keys. The distance from George's to the pub is a two-figure number of miles, and the two digits in reverse order give the distance of the pub from their daughter's.

How far is it from George's home to the Crossed Keys?

48 | FOOTBALL FANS

The clubs Barnet, Exeter, Gillingham, Plymouth, Southend and Walsall need to attract more fans. So each has persuaded one of the players Aguero, Ibrahimovic, Lampard, Neymar, Schweinsteiger and Suarez to join them. Also, each club has persuaded one of the managers Conte, Mourinho, Pellegrini, Terim, Van Gaal and Wenger to take control. For each club, if you look at the club, player and manager, then for any two of the three there are just two different letters of the alphabet that occur in both (with the letters possibly occurring more than once).

In alphabetical order of the teams, list their new players.

49 | ALL SAINTS DAY

I have written down three even numbers and then consistently replaced digits by letters with different letters used for different digits. In this way I get:

ALL THE SAINTS

In fact multiplying together the first two of these numbers gives the third.

What number is my SAINT?

50 | MADAM I'M ADAM

Adam noticed that today's Teaser number was a four-figure palindrome. He told me that he had written down another four-figure palindrome and he asked me to guess what it was. I asked for some clues regarding its prime factors and so he told me, in turn, whether his number was divisible by 2, 3, 5, 7, 11, 13, ... Only after he had told me whether it was divisible by 13 was it possible to work out his number.

What was his number?

51 | KING LEAR III

King Lear III had a square kingdom divided into sixteen equal-sized smaller square plots, numbered in the usual way. He decided to keep a realm for himself and share the rest into equal realms (larger than his) for his daughters, a "realm" being a collection of one or more connected plots. He chose a suitable realm for himself and one for his eldest daughter and he noticed that, in each case, multiplying together any plot numbers within the realm gave a perfect square. Then he found that there was only one way to divide the remainder of the kingdom into suitable realms.

List the plot numbers of the eldest daughter's realm and of the king's realm.

52 | LOADED DICE

I have two traditional-looking dice, but only one of them is fair. In the other there is an equal chance of getting a 1, 2, 3, 4 or 5, but the dice is loaded so that a 6 is thrown more than half the time. I threw the two dice and noted the total. It turned out that with my dice the chance of getting that total was double what it would have been with two fair dice.

What (as a simple fraction) is the chance of getting a 6 with the loaded dice?

53 | STRICTLY NOT

Four celebrities entered a dance competition. Five judges each shared out their eight marks among the four dancers, with each getting a non-zero whole number. Each judge split the eight marks in a different way and then allocated them as follows. Amanda's marks to Lana and Natasha added to the same total as Barry's marks to Madge and Paula. Barry gave more marks to Madge than to any other dancer, Charles gave more to Paula than to any other, and Doris gave more to Natasha than to any other. Lana scored more from Edna than from Amanda. All dancers had the same total so the head judge's scores were used, giving a winner and runner-up.

Who was the head judge, who was the winner and who was the runner-up?

54 | WINNING MONTHS

I have won three Premium Bond prizes and noted the number of non-winning months between my first and second wins, and also the number between my second and third wins. Looking at the letters in the spelling of the months, I have also noted the difference between the numbers of letters in the months of my first and second wins, and also the difference between those of the months of my second and third wins. All four numbers noted were the same, and if you knew that number then it would be possible to work out the months of my wins.

What (in order of the wins) were those three months?

55 | SUMMING UP 2015

I asked Harry and Tomto to write down three numbers that between them used nine different digits and which added to 2015. They each succeeded and one of Harry's three numbers was the same as one of Tom's. I noticed that Harry's three numbers included a perfect square and Tom's included a higher perfect square.

What were those two squares?

56 | COLD TURKEY

We are having a "cold turkey" party on Boxing Day. Fewer than 100 people have indicated that they are coming, and the percentage of them choosing the vegetarian option is (to the nearest whole number) a single-digit number. My vegetarian aunt might also come. If she does, then (to the nearest whole number) the percentage having the vegetarian option will remain the same.

If she does come, how many people will be there and how many of them will have the vegetarian option?

57 | NEW YEAR PARTY

We have a game planned for our forthcoming New Year party. Each person there will write their name on a slip of paper and the slips will be shuffled and one given to each person. If anyone gets their own slip, then all the slips will be collected up and we shall start again. When everyone has been given a name different from their own, each person will use their right hand to hold the left hand of the person named on their slip. We hope that everyone will then be forming one circle ready to sing Auld Lang Syne – but there's a slightly less than evens chance of this happening.

How many people will there be at the party?

58 | CALENDAR DICE

I have tried to make a calendar using some dice. To display the month I want to use three dice, with a capital letter on each of the faces to display:

J A N or F E B or M A R etc

I chose the capital letters on the dice to enable me to go as far as possible through the year. Furthermore, it turned out that one particular dice contained four vowels.

(a) What was the last month that I was able to display?

(b) What were the two other letters on that particular dice?

59 | NUMBER TIME

I have written down some numbers and then consistently replaced digits by capital letters, with different letters used for different digits. In this way my numbers have become:

TRIPLE (which is a multiple of three)

EIGHT (which is a cube)

NINE (which is divisible by nine)

PRIME (which is a prime)

What is the number TIME?

60 | SPIDERS

Spiders Beth and Sam wake up in the bottom corner of a cuboidal barn (all of whose sides are whole numbers of metres). They want to reach the opposite bottom corner without actually walking across the floor. Beth decides to walk on one of five possible shortest routes, two of them being around the edge of the floor and the other three being over the walls and ceiling. Sam decides instead to spin a web directly to the point on the ceiling diagonally opposite the starting point and then to drop down into the corner.

The total length of his journey is within five centimetres of a whole number of metres. How high is the barn?

61 | OLD BOYS' BANQUET

George and Martha have arranged the seating plan for the annual Old Boys banquet; it involves a number of tables, each seating 50 diners. More than half the Old Boys are bringing one female guest each and the rest are coming alone. Martha wrote down three numbers, namely the number of Old Boys bringing a guest, the number of Old Boys coming alone, and the total number of Old Boys coming. George noted that the three numbers between them used each of the digits 0 to 9 exactly once.

How many Old Boys are bringing a guest, and how many are coming alone?

62 | THREE LIVES

I think of a whole number from 1 to 20 inclusive and Andy has to try to guess the number. He starts with three lives and makes successive guesses: after each guess I tell him whether it is right or too low or too high. If it is too high he loses one of his lives. To win the game he has to guess my number before his lives run out. He has developed the best possible strategy and can always win with a certain number of guesses or fewer. In fact no-one could be sure of winning with fewer guesses than that "certain number".

What is that "certain number"?

63 | UNCLE'S GIFT (1)

Uncle Bill has sent a whole number of pounds (less than fifty) to be shared among his three nephews Tom, Dick and Harry. Each has received a whole number of pounds, with Tom receiving the most and Harry the least, but with Tom getting less than twice as much as Harry. Each boy's fraction of the total gift, when expressed as a decimal, consists of three digits recurring (as in .abcabc...), and the nine digits that appear in the three decimals are all different. (Uncle Ben also sent some money, but I'll tell you about that next month.)

How much did Tom, Dick and Harry get from Uncle Bill?

64 | OUT OF ORDER

I have written down five positive whole numbers whose sum is less than 100. If you wrote the numbers in words, then you would find that each of them begins with a different letter of the alphabet. (Surprisingly, the same is true of the five numbers obtained by increasing each of my five numbers by one.) If you write my five numbers in words and put them in alphabetical order, then they will be in decreasing order.

What (in decreasing order) are my five numbers?

65 | CRIME-WRITERS CONVENTION

A group of twelve crime writers attended a convention. They were Bonfiglioli, Durrenmatt, Fyfield, Hiaasen, Highsmith, Hill, Innes, James, Knox, Le Carre, Rendell and Sayers. They sat in one long row on the stage, with Hiaasen further to the left than Hill. It turned out that, for any two sitting next to each other, there was just one letter of the alphabet that occurred (perhaps more than once) in both their surnames.

List the initial of each author from left to right along the row.

66 | RED-LETTER DAYS

The months of my 2016 calendar are headed M, T, W, Th, F, Sa, Su, with the dates 1, 2, 3 ... in a grid of squares underneath. I have shaded all the days on which I have meetings planned – all of them being on weekdays. For example, in February the days 1, 2, 3, 4, 8 and 9 are shaded: these shaded squares form a connected piece and the product of the numbers is a perfect cube. The same is true of the shaded squares in another month – and in fact it's the largest possible such cube in the calendar. My last meeting in that month is on my aunt's birthday.

What is her birthday?

67 | UNCLE'S GIFT (2)

Last month I told you about Uncle Bill's gifts to his nephews. Uncle Ben has also sent a whole number of pounds (less than fifty) to be shared among his three nephews Tom, Dick and Harry. Each has received a different whole number of pounds, with Tom receiving the most and Harry the least, but with Tom getting less than twice as much as Harry. Each boy's fraction of the total gift, when expressed as a decimal, consists of three different digits recurring (as in .abcabc...), and each boy's decimal uses the same three digits.

How much did Tom, Dick and Harry get from Uncle Ben?

68 | FACTOIDELS

In order to introduce the class to "lowest common denominators", Amelia's teacher asked them to find the lowest number with the property that each of 1, 2, 3, 4 and 5 divided exactly into it. They correctly calculated the answer as 60, and the teacher called this the "factoidel" of 5. He went on to demonstrate that the factoidel of 6 was also 60. Being keen, Amelia investigated factoidels at home and then told the teacher that she had found the highest set of four consecutive numbers whose factoidels are all different (at least she had cleverly checked well into the billions).

What were those four consecutive numbers?

69 | FOUR-SQUARE FAMILY

My four sons are all under 20 and just one of them is a teenager. Their ages (or, more precisely, the squares of their ages) have some remarkable properties. Firstly, two years ago the square of one of their ages equalled the sum of the squares of the other three ages. Secondly, this year the sum of the squares of two of their ages equals the sum of the squares of the other two ages.

What, in increasing order, are their ages?

70 | EASTER TEASER

I have written down three numbers and then consistently replaced digits by letters, with different letters for different digits, to give:

EASTER SUNDAY TEASER

In fact the first number is the lowest and one of these numbers is the sum of the other two.

What is this SUNDAY's number?

71 | SUM TRIANGLES

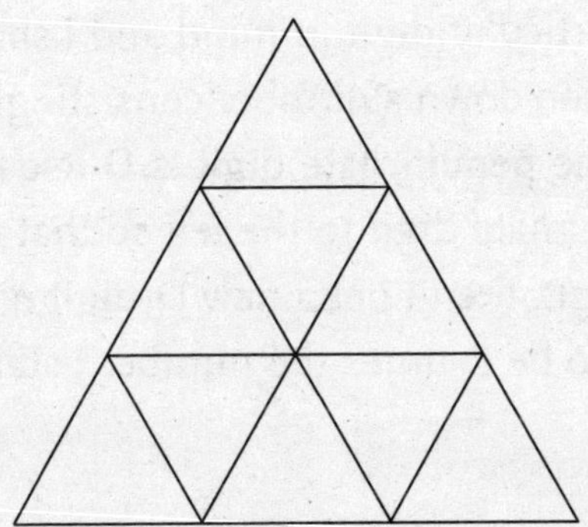

The number of upwardly-pointing triangles (of all sizes) visible in this picture is ten. Trix has drawn a similar arrangement but with lots more rows: the number of small upward-pointing triangles in her bottom row is equal to her age and the total of upward-pointing triangles that can be seen is divisible by any of the digits 1 to 9.

How old is Trix?

72 | D-DAY

I have a particular digit in mind and I shall call it D. I have written down a number consisting of D digits in which the penultimate digit is D itself. If I move that penultimate digit to the left so that it becomes the first digit, then I get a new D-digit number that turns out to be D times the number I started with.

What is the D-digit number I started with?

73 | NO MEAN FEAT

I bought a run of consecutively numbered raffle tickets, some of which were red and the rest were blue. Among my numbers no red number was the average of two other reds, and no blue number was the average of two other blues. I actually won the raffle. My two-figure winning red number was in fact the geometric mean of two other red numbers of mine. [The geometric mean of M and N is the square root of MxN.]

What were my blue numbers?

74 | GEORGE AND THE DRAGON

Yesterday was St George's day and to celebrate George getting even with the dragon I wrote down an addition sum. Then I replaced digits consistently by letters, using different letters for different digits, to give:

SAINT + GEORGE = DRAGON

Given that GEORGE is even, what number is DRAGON?

75 | SUNDAY TIMES TABLE

Do you remember reciting your "times tables" – for example, "one seven is 7, two sevens are 14, three sevens are 21", continuing 28, 35, ... and going on forever? I have consistently replaced some digits by letters and in this way the five-figure number TIMES can be found in the times table of each of its digits but not in the times table of any other digit. On the other hand, TABLE can be found in the times table of seven different digits, each of which is a digit of TIMES or TABLE.

What number would be BEST?

76 | HOUSEY-HOUSEY

Philip, Daphne and I live in different houses on Teaser Drive. Philip lives at number 1 and the houses are then numbered consecutively along one side of the road. The sum of the house numbers strictly between Philip's house and mine is equal to the sum of the house numbers strictly between my house and Daphne's. Furthermore, the digits of Daphne's house number add up to the same total as the digits of my house number.

What is my house number and what is Daphne's?

77 | DESERT PATROL

Pat is at Base Camp in the desert. There is enough fuel at the base for his vehicle to travel 420 miles, but the vehicle can hold (in its tank and in cans) at most enough fuel for 105 miles. On any journey he can leave some fuel in cans at any point and then pick up some or all of it whenever he passes in future. He has worked out that there is just enough fuel for him to reach the Main Camp.

How far is it between the two camps?

78 | PROMOTING RUGBY

Six male rugby players and six female rugby players are helping to promote the game. The men are Eastmond, Morgan, Twelvetrees, Webber, Yarde and Youngs. The women are Allen, Clarke, Croker, McGilchrist, McLean and Thompson. The men have paired off with the women and one pair has gone to each of the counties East Sussex, Hampshire, Isle of Wight, Norfolk, Suffolk and Surrey. For each pair, if you look at the name of the man, the name of the woman and the name of their county, then for any two of the three names just two different letters of the alphabet occur in both (possibly more than once).

The men above are listed in alphabetical order: in that order, who are their female partners?

79 | END OF SEASON

In this football league each team plays each of the others once (with three points for a win and one for a draw). The end-of-season table has teams in decreasing order of points (ties being determined by goals scored). Here are some of the entries from three rows of the table, but with digits consistently replaced by letters.

	Points	Won	Drawn	Lost	Goals scored	Goals against
United		M	Y			
Villa	T	E	A	S	E	R
Wanderers			T	I	M	E

How many teams are in the league, and what was the score when Villa played Wanderers?

80 | THAT'S THE TICKET!

Alan, Betty and Charlie each chose a different set of six numbers (from 1 to 49) for their lottery ticket. In each case the product of the six numbers was a perfect square and also each set of six numbers used each of the digits 0 to 9 exactly once.

Alan won the lottery by getting all six numbers correct. Betty and Charlie also got prizes because they each had at least three numbers correct.

What were Alan's six numbers?

81 | EASY AS ABC

George and Martha have replaced the digits 0 to 9 by the letters A to J in some order. George then noted a neat product, namely:

$$AB \times CDE = FGHIJ$$

Then Martha noted a neat sum, namely:

$$AB + CD + EF + GH + IJ = CCC$$

What, in order, are the values of the letters A to J?

82 | SPOTS BEFORE THE EYES

At the opticians I was shown a sequence of six screens. On each there was a different number of spots ranging from 0 to 5 and I had to say how many I thought I could see. This was done with the left eye and then repeated with the right. The optician always used the same sequence and my answers were 5 2 3 4 4 3 and 4 1 4 5 2 3.

In each case I got two correct. When I asked if this was the worst he'd seen, the optician showed me these three earlier sets of answers in which just one was correct in each: 2 2 1 2 1 4 and 3 3 2 3 5 1 and 0 4 5 1 3 2.

What was the correct sequence?

83 | GREEK URNS

I have three Greek urns. I took some balls (consisting of an odd number of red balls and some black balls) and I placed one or more ball in the first urn, one or more in the second, and the rest in the third. If you chose an urn at random and then a ball at random from that urn, then overall there would be a 50 per cent chance of getting a red ball.

Then I moved some black balls from one of the urns to another. In this new situation, if you chose an urn and then a ball there was a 75 per cent chance of getting a red. In fact, with this set of balls and urns it would be impossible to get a higher percentage than that.

How many red balls and how many black balls were there?

84 | JACK'S JIGSAW

I made Jack a jigsaw. I started with a rectangle of card that I had cut from an A4 sheet and then I cut the rectangle into pieces. There were some square pieces of sizes (in centimetres) 1 1, 2´2, 3´3, ... with the largest having side equal to Jack's age. The remaining pieces were rectangles of sizes 1´2, 2´3, 3´4, ... with the largest length among them again being Jack's age. Then Jack succeeded in putting them together again to form a rectangle, but the perimeter of his rectangle was smaller than the perimeter of my original rectangle.

What were the lengths of the sides of my original rectangle?

85 | PENTAGONS

I have taken five identical straight rods and joined each to the next by a hinge to make a flexible ring. With this ring I can make lots of different pentagonal shapes, and in particular I can make lots of pentagons with area equal to a whole number of square centimetres. The largest whole-numbered area achievable is a two-figure number, and the smallest whole-numbered area achievable is another two-figure number. In fact these two numbers use the same two digits but in the reverse order.

What is the largest whole-numbered area achievable?

86 | HOT STUFF

George and Martha are dabbling in the world of high temperature physics. George was measuring the temperature of a molten metal and wrote down the result. He thought this was in degrees Centigrade and so he converted it to Fahrenheit. However, Martha pointed out that the original result was already in degrees Fahrenheit and so George converted it to Centigrade. Martha wrote down the original result and each of George's two calculated answers. She noted that they were all four-figure numbers and that their sum was palindromic.

What was the original four-figure result?

87 | THIS AND THAT

I have written down a list of eleven numbers and then consistently replaced digits by letters, with different letters for different digits. In this way the list becomes:

SO DO WHAT NOW

ADD AND SEND IN THIS AND THAT

The grand total of these eleven numbers is a four-figure number.

Numerically, what is THIS + THAT?

88 | ALMOST A YEAR APART

Tomorrow's date is 1st August 2016, which in the usual six-digit format is 01 08 16. This can be regarded as a 'square' date since 10816 is a perfect square. No square date is followed by another square date exactly one year later, although some pairs of square dates are very nearly one year apart.

Which two square dates (in their six-digit format) come closest to being a year apart?

89 | MAKING ARRANGEMENTS

Beth wrote down a three-figure number and she also listed the five other three-figure numbers that could be made using those same three digits. Then she added up the six numbers: it gave a total whose digits were all different, and none of those digits appeared in her original number.

If you knew whether her original number was prime or not, and you knew whether the sum of the three digits of her original number was prime or not, then it would be possible to work out her number.

What was it?

90 | SUM CARD TRICK

Joe has nine cards, white on one side and grey on the other, with a single digit written on each side of each card. He gave them to Penny to arrange white-side-up to form three three-figure numbers with the sum of the first two equalling the third. This was her attempt:

2 1 9 6 5 4 8 7 3

Then Joe turned the cards over one at a time to reveal

9 8 7 1 4 2 3 6 5

where the total of the first two did not equal the third. So he challenged Penny to arrange the cards so that both white-side-up and grey-side-up the third number was the sum of the first two, which she did.

What was her third grey number?

91 | KATY'S PIGGY BANKS

Our granddaughter Katy has two piggy banks containing a mixture of 10p and 50p coins, making a grand total of £10. The first piggy bank contains less than the other, and in it the number of 50p coins is a multiple of the number of 10p coins.

Katy chose a coin at random from the first piggy bank and then put it in the second. Then she chose a coin at random from the second and put it in the first. She ended up with the same amount of money in the first piggy bank as when she started. In fact there was a 50:50 chance of this happening.

How much did she end up with in the first piggy bank?

92 | TODAY'S TEASER

Today's Teaser concerns writing a date as a string of six digits: for example, today's date can be written as 280816. Our puzzle concerns two numbers that add up to a date. I have written down two six-figure numbers and then consistently replaced digits by letters. In this way the two numbers have become:

TODAYS TEASER

The sum of these two numbers equals the six-digit date of a Sunday in July, August or September this year.

What is the value of my TEASER?

93 | PIN-IN-THE-MIDDLE

For Max Stout's various accounts and cards he has nine different four-digit PINs to remember. For security reasons none of them is the multiple of another, and none is an anagram of another. He has written these PINs in a three-by-three array with one PIN in each place in the array.

It turns out that the product of the three PINs in any row, column or main diagonal is the same. In fact there are just two different prime numbers that divide into this product.

What is the PIN in the middle position of the array?

94 | CHAT SHOWS

Each day next week there will be a chat show on television and in each show the host will appear with an actress and an actor. The hosts will be (in order) Dimbleby, Evans, Mack, Marr, Norton, Peschardt and Ross. In no particular order, the actresses will be Arterton, Blunt, Carter, Jones, Knightley, Margolyes and Watson. Again in no particular order, the actors will be Bean, Caine, Cleese, Craig, De Niro, Neeson and Oldman. For any two people in the same show there are just two different letters of the alphabet that occur (perhaps more than once) in both their surnames.

List the actresses in the order in which they appear.

95 | OUR SECRET

Eight friends joined a very secret society and each was given a different membership number between 70 and 100. The friends are Bec, Cal, Doc, Ian, Jon, Luv, Rev and one other – and I am not willing to divulge his common three-letter name. But I can tell you that his membership number is 84. Also, Bec's membership number is the highest of the eight. The friends noticed that, for any pair of them, their names had at least one letter in common if and only if their membership numbers had a common prime factor.

(a) What was Ian's membership number?
(b) What was the name of the eighth friend?

96 | ACCOUNTABILITY

George and Martha's bank account number is an eight-digit number consisting of the digits 1 to 8 in some order. Martha commented that, if you split the number into two four-figure numbers, then the number formed by the last four digits is a multiple of the number formed by the first four digits. Then George listed all the different prime numbers that divided exactly into the account number. When he added together all those primes the total was less than a hundred.

What is their account number?

97 | AN AGE-OLD PROBLEM

Five men of different ages under fifty are celebrating their joint birthday in the pub. Alan's age is the average of their five ages. When Bob is three times Alan's age today, the sum of Alan's and Colin's ages will equal the sum of their five ages today. Furthermore, Derek will then be three times his age today, and Eric will be one year more than double Bob's age today.

The landlord checked that the youngest of the five was allowed to buy alcohol.

Who is the youngest, and how old is he?

98 | TEN DIGITS

Without repeating a digit I have written down three numbers, all greater than one. Each number contains a different number of digits. If I also write down the product of all three numbers, then the total number of digits I have used is ten. The product contains two pairs of different digits, neither of which appear in the three original numbers.

What is the product?

99 | MAGIC CARDS

Joe placed nine cards on the table to form the magic square shown on the left below (where each row, column and diagonal has the same total). Then he turned over each card one at a time and the result is shown on the right below: it is not magic.

4	11	9		7	4	8
13	8	3		3	6	9
7	5	12		2	14	1

Penny then rearranged the cards to form a magic square which, after each card was turned over, was also magic.

What (in increasing order) were the four corner numbers in her magic square with the higher total?

100 | LOSING WEIGHT

The members of our local sports club are split into two groups. Originally the groups had the same number of members, and the first group contained member Waites who weighed 100kg (and indeed that was the average weight of the members of the first group). Then the club trainer decided that the groups were overweight and that, for each of the next ten weeks, for each group the average weight of the members should be reduced by one kilogram.

This was achieved by simply transferring a member from the first group to the second group each week, and Waites was the tenth member to be transferred.

How many members are there in the club?

101 | QUEUING

Tickets for the event went on sale at 09:30. The queue started at 09:00 when two people arrived, then four more at 09:01, six more at 09:02 and so on until 60 more arrived at 09:29. Just 16 people arrived at 09:30, 16 more at 09:31, 16 more at 09:32 and so on. Tickets were sold at 25 per minute (with one to each person in the queue) until they were sold out. Joe and I both had identical waiting times before being sold our tickets, despite me having arrived earlier, and no-one who got a ticket waited for less time than us.

At what time did Joe join the queue?

102 | NEW EXTENSION

George has just moved departments and he has a new four-figure telephone extension number. He shows it to Martha and proudly points out that, if you delete any two of the digits of the extension number, then the remaining two-figure number is prime. Martha then lists the resulting six different primes and comments delightedly that more than one of them divides exactly into the extension number.

What is George's new extension number?

103 | TWIN SETS

The twins Wunce and Repete each made a list of positive perfect squares. In Wunce's list each of the digits 0 to 9 was used exactly once, whereas in Repete's list each of the digits was used at least once. Wunce commented that the sum of his squares equalled their year of birth, and Repete responded by saying that the sum of his squares was less than the square of their age.

What is the sum of Wunce's squares, and what is the sum of Repete's?

104 | BY HECK!

The registration number of my old car consists of three consecutive letters of the alphabet in reverse order, followed by a three-figure number consisting of the same digit written three times, followed finally by a single letter.

I am a fan of "hex" (ie, arithmetic in base 16, with "digits" 0, 1, 2, 3, 4, 5, 6, 7, 8, 9, A, B, C, D, E and F) and I realised that the registration number looked like a number in hex. So I worked out its equivalent value in our usual base-10 arithmetic. Miraculously the answer was a nine-figure number that used all nine of the non-zero digits.

What is the registration number?

105 | PASSWORD

My computer password consists of different digits written in decreasing order.

I can rearrange the digits to form a perfect cube.

A further rearrangement gives a perfect square.

Another rearrangement gives a prime number.

A further rearrangement gives a number that is divisible by the number of digits in the password.

Yet another rearrangement gives a number that is divisible by all but one of its digits.

What is my password?

106 | RETURN TO ZENDA

Each postcode in Ruritania consists of ten digits, the first three showing the area, the next three showing the town, and the final four showing the house. Just twelve houses have "lucky" postcodes that have no repeated digit and which consist of two three-figure squares followed by a four-figure square. Rudolph lives in such a house and he recently met a girl called Flavia. She only told him that hers was the only house in her area with a lucky postcode, and that her area/town/house numbers were all bigger than his. He has found a postcode satisfying these conditions and sent her a Christmas card, but it has been returned as it was not her postcode.

What is Rudolph's postcode?

107 | MAKING A DOZEN

In this addition sum different letters stand consistently for different digits:

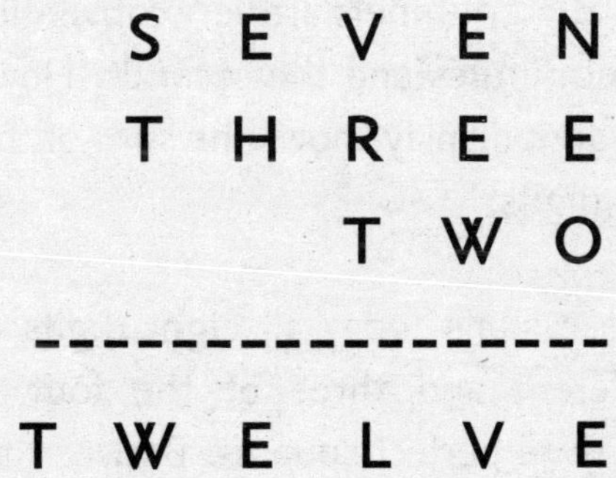

What is the value of LETTERS?

108 | TIME FOR CHRISTMAS

For Christmas George has bought Martha a novelty digital 24-hour clock. It has an eight-digit display forming four two-digit numbers. The first three of these two-digit numbers are very conventional – the hours, the minutes and the seconds. However, the final two-digit display shows the sum of the first six displayed digits!

On two occasions today all eight digits displayed were different and three of the four two-digit numbers were perfect squares. Between those two occasions there was a time when the eight digits displayed were again all different, but this time the sum of the eight digits was a perfect square!

What was the eight-digit display at that in-between time?

109 | NINE LADIES DANCING

On the ninth day of Christmas the ladies Anne, Bella, Cary, Debbie, Eileen, Fran, Gill, Honor and Iris entered a dancing competition. In some order they had labels 'One', 'Two', 'Three', 'Four', 'Five', 'Six', 'Seven', 'Eight' and 'Nine' on their backs. They each danced a different dance chosen from cha-cha, charleston, foxtrot, jive, polka, quickstep, samba, twist and waltz.

For any lady's name and label there was just one letter of the alphabet that occurred (once or more) in both. The same was true for any lady's name and their dance, and also for any lady's label and dance.

In alphabetical order of their names, what are the numbers of the nine ladies?

110 | A NEW YEAR REMINISCENCE

Whilst filing away last year's diary this morning I came across an old diary from my teenage years. In it I can see that in one particular month I went to four parties, three of them being on Saturdays and the other on a Sunday. I wrote down the four dates of the parties in words (in the format "January first" etc) and found that each of the dates used a different prime number of letters.

What were the four dates that I wrote down?

111 | CELEBRITY DOGS

Six celebrities appeared on television with their dogs. Each celebrity brought two dogs and between them they had twelve different breeds.

The celebrities were Clooney, Hathaway, Jackman, Palermo, Rossum and Seyfried. The breeds of dog were Akita, Basenji, Basset, Bull Terrier, Chihuahua, Dalmation, Foxhound, Keeshond, Plott, Poodle, Rottweiler and Setter.

For the name and breeds in each trio of celebrity plus their two dogs, if you look at any two out of the three then there are just two letters of the alphabet that occur (once or more) in both.

In alphabetical order of the breeds, please list the initials of the owners (e.g. C, S, A, C, ...)

112 | DEGREES OF FREEDOM

I bought an odd thermometer from an old curiosity shop. On its linear scale the freezing point and boiling point of water were higher than they are on the centigrade scale. In fact the freezing point was a prime number and, higher up the scale, the boiling point was a perfect square. There was only one number on the scale where it actually agreed with the corresponding centigrade temperature. That number was the negative of an odd prime (and not the same prime as the one mentioned earlier).

On this new scale, what are the freezing and boiling points of water?

113 | JEWELLER'S ROUGE

Fabulé's latest creation consists of a set of equal-sized silver cubes. On each face of each cube there is one diagonal of identical rubies. No two cubes are the same, but had Fabulé made any more such cubes then it would have been necessary to repeat one of the designs.

How many cubes are there in the set?

114 | SQUARING UP

Alice had a large collection of one centimetre square tiles. She used them to make a set of some larger squares of different sizes, all with sides of less than a metre. When I saw these squares I removed one corner tile from each. Then, for each mutilated shape, Alice moved the minimum number of tiles to transform it into a rectangle. Overall she moved two hundred tiles. This resulted in a set of rectangles all of whose sides were a prime number of centimetres long.

What (in increasing order) were the lengths of the sides of her original squares?

115 | BACK AND FORTH

George and Martha have a digital 24-hour clock that always displays the time as four digits (eg, 0217).

During one lazy weekend George noted two particular times when the four-digit display was palindromic. He calculated the number of minutes from the first of these times to the second and he discovered that the answer was a three-figure palindrome. When he reported all the details to Martha, she commented that the sum of the eleven digits in the three palindromes was also palindromic.

What were the two palindromic times?

116 | KING LEAR IV

King Lear IV's realm consisted of a regular hexagon divided into 24 counties that were equal-sized equilateral triangles. In his will he wanted to share the counties among his six daughters, each daughter's portion having the property that, if you walked in a straight line between any two points in it, then you remained in her portion. If two daughters' portions had the same area then they had to be of different shapes (and not the mirror image of each other). He wanted Cordelia to have a single county (his favourite county on the edge of the kingdom), he wanted Goneril to have a hexagonal-shaped portion, and he knew the number of counties he wanted to allocate to each of the other daughters, with Reagan's portion being the largest of all. It turned out that his requirements uniquely determined Goneril's and Reagan's counties.

What, in increasing order, were the numbers of counties allocated to the six daughters?

117 | UNWHOLESOME

I have written down three positive numbers, the highest of which is an even two-figure number. Also, one of the numbers is the average of the other two. I have calculated the product of the three numbers and the answer is a prime number. You might be surprised that the product of three numbers is a prime but, of course, they are not all whole numbers – at least one of them is a fraction.

What is the largest of the three numbers, and what is the product of the three?

118 | SIGNS OF THE TIMES

I was taking a gentle morning drive along the straight road to Secombe that passes through Firsk. Before reaching Firsk I passed three signposts, each giving the distances to Firsk and to Secombe (to the nearest mile). All six distances displayed were different and, amazingly, all were perfect squares.

What were the two distances given on the first signpost (furthest from Firsk)?

119 | CRENELLATION AGGREGATION

The castle's crenellated outer walls formed a pentagon, and on a family visit we decided to count the crenels. My son counted the number on each side and found that these totals were five consecutive two-figure numbers. My daughter and wife started together and then one of them walked clockwise around the walls and the other walked anticlockwise. They each counted the crenels they passed until they met. Their totals were two different prime numbers (with no prime number between the two). I consulted the tourist leaflet and found that the total number of crenels was in fact the product of three prime numbers.

How many crenels were there in total?

120 | THE BEST POLICY

George and Martha's home insurance policy number is a six-figure number consisting of six different digits. George commented that the number was divisible by each of its digits and also by the sum of its digits. Martha then added that if you deleted the left-hand digit then you were left with a five-figure number divisible by the sum of its five digits. If you then deleted that number's left-hand digit, then you were left with a four-figure number divisible by the sum of its four digits, and so on all the way down.

What is their policy number?

121 | CHILD'S PLAY

Liam has a set of cards numbered from 1 to 12. He can lay some or all of these in a row to form various numbers. For example the four cards

6 8 11 2

give a five-figure number. Also, that particular number is exactly divisible by the number on each of the cards used.

In this way Liam used his set of cards to find another much larger number that was divisible by each of the numbers on the cards used – in fact he found the largest such possible number.

What was that number?

122 | IMPRISMED

A right regular prism has two ends with identical faces, joined by oblong rectangular faces. I have eight of them, with regular convex polygonal end-faces of 3, 4, 5, 6, 7, 8, 9 and 10 sides (triangle, square and so on). They sit on my flat desk (on oblong faces), and each prism has the same height.

I chose three prisms at random, and was able to slide them into contact, broadside, in such a way that the middle one overhung both others (and could be lifted without disturbing them). Also, I was able to slide one outer prism to the other side, and the new "middle" prism was overhung by both others (and so vertically "imprisoned" by them).

I was able to do all this again with three randomly chosen remaining prisms.

Give the prior chance of this double selection (as a fraction in lowest terms).

123 | BALED OUT

In my fantasy Euro football championship the four home teams were in the same group, with each team playing each other team once. Group positions were decided on points, then using "goal differences" and then "goals scored" if necessary.

After having played two games each, just three goals had been scored in the group, leading to England being ahead with Northern Ireland second, Scotland third and Wales fourth. Wales realised that they had to score at least three goals in their remaining game in order to have a chance of being group leaders. In the final game of the group, Bale scored a third goal in the dying seconds, resulting in Wales being group winners and knocking England into second place.

What were the scores in the six games (in the order EvN, EvS, EvW, NvS, NvW, SvW)?

124 | BINGO!

The infant teacher played a bingo game with his class. He had two identical dice, the numbers on the six faces of each being 1, 2, 2, 3, 3 and 3. He told the class that he would throw the pair of dice, add up the two numbers showing, and call that number out in a game of bingo. He then asked each member of the class to make their own bingo card consisting of five numbers of their own choice. He explained that they could repeat a number on their card if they wished (and then delete just one occurrence of the number whenever it was called). Most of the class chose the five possible different totals as their bingo numbers, but one very clever girl chose the best possible selection.

What were her five numbers?

125 | EASTER PARADE

Following the success of last year's Easter parade our village is going to make it an annual event. To celebrate today's parade I have taken three numbers and I have consistently replaced digits by letters to give:

ANNUAL EASTER PARADE

In fact the third number is the sum of the other two.

What is the number PARADE?

126 | COFFEE BREAKS

The roads on our estate form a grid consisting of three roads running west-to-east with a number of other roads running south-to-north from the bottom road across the middle road to the top road.

I live at the south-west corner of the grid and I work at the north-east corner. Each day I walk to work by one of the various shortest possible routes along the roads: there is a two-figure number of such routes. One quarter of my possible routes pass Caffee Claudius, and one quarter of my routes pass Spenda Coffee (which are on different roads).

How many of my routes pass both the coffee shops?

127 | SWIFT TAILOR

When measuring a gentleman's chest size in inches, the tailor's five-foot long tape overlapped so that the set of numbers from 1 to 9 was aligned with a consecutive set of higher numbers. Taking each pair of these nine aligned lower and higher numbers as a fraction, the tailor saw that just two of the nine "fractions" were in their simplest form and did not cancel down (ie, the pair of numbers had no common factor greater than 1).

All of this was also true when he measured the smaller waist size.

What (in inches) were the gentleman's chest and waist sizes?

128 | ON COURSE

Hackers-on-Sea golf course is designed by the great Jack Arnold. It is a par-seventy course and its eighteen holes are all par three, four or five. The numbers of all the par-five holes are primes, and the numbers of the par-four holes are odd.

Recently I only had time to play half the course and ideally my nine consecutive holes should be par thirty-five. However, there is no such collection of holes.

What are the numbers of the par-four holes?

129 | KNOWING THE LINGO

A group of 64 students can speak, between them, French, German and Russian. There are three times as many French speakers and two times as many German speakers as there are Russian speakers. The number who speak all three languages is one fifth of the number who speak French and at least one other of these languages. The number who speak all three languages is also two ninths of the number who speak German and at least one other of these languages. Furthermore, the number who speak all three languages is also two fifths of the number who speak Russian and at least one other of these languages.

How many of the 64 students speak only French?

130 | WHEN IN ROME

An ancient five-by-five table of letters been found in Rome. All the ten different five-letter rows across and five-letter columns down are Roman numerals, with no letter exceeding a C. The across numbers are, in order, even, even, a cube, a prime, and a power of 2. The down numbers include a cube, the rest being even or prime.

Which two Roman numerals cross at the middle square?

131 | MARBLE MARVEL

I had a cuboid (or rectangular block) of marble whose volume in cubic centimetres was divisible by each of the numbers 1, 2, 3, 4, 5, 6, 7, 8 and 9. Unfortunately I dropped the block and it broke into two cuboids, and surprisingly the two new blocks were of similar shape to each other (ie, one was a magnification of the other). The lengths of the sides of the original block and the two new blocks were all two-figure numbers of centimetres.

What were the lengths of the sides of the original block?

132 | POWER SURGE

I recently checked my energy bills. I noticed that the account numbers for my electricity and gas are two different six-figure numbers, and that one is a multiple of the other. The electricity account number is a perfect cube and the sum of its digits is a perfect square. The gas account number is a perfect square (and, as it happens, the sum of its digits is a perfect cube!).

What is the gas account number?

133 | FAB FOUR

Here are four numbers, where each is the same fixed whole-number multiple of the previous one. However, in some places I have consistently replaced digits by letters – and in the other places the digits have been replaced by dashes. In this way the numbers have become the fabulous four:

JOHN P-UL R---O ----GE

What number is my GROUP?

134 | SOLID JELLOMETRY

As a wedding gift, Granny Lucci gave us a set of five jelly moulds, which was odd in many ways. The base of each mould was a different regular polygon (including a triangle) with each side an odd number of centimetres in length. Each polygon had the same length perimeter, an odd two-figure number of centimetres.

The sides of the moulds were vertical and the heights of the moulds were all the same odd number of centimetres. The volumes of the moulds were all between one litre and two litres.

What was the height of the moulds?

135 | SIGNIFICANT ERRORS

Last year George and Martha were going to visit one of their daughters. Her house number was a two-figure number but unfortunately Martha wrote the number incorrectly by making the first digit less than it should be. When George discovered the error he commented that the incorrect number was a whole number percentage of the correct one. If you knew that percentage then you should be able to work out their daughter's house number. Then the daughter moved to a different two-figure house number, Martha again wrote the number incorrectly by making the first digit less than it should be, and again the incorrect number was a whole number percentage of the correct one. If you knew that percentage then you should be able to work out their daughter's new house number.

What was the daughter's original house number, and what is the new one?

136 | BEACH GAME

Ken, Leanne, Mike, Nancy, Olive and Paul were playing on the beach. They had drawn a large circle in the sand and written their names clockwise, in that order, equally spaced around the edge of the circle. They also had a circular piece of card around which they had written the numbers 1 to 6 clockwise in order, also equally spaced. Then they spun the card in the middle of the sand circle and each child was awarded the number of points equal to the number closest to their name. They kept repeating this process and after each spin they kept a total of their scores so far. Mike was ahead after the first spin and after each of the first five spins there was a different clear leader. Then the tide came in and washed the game away.

Which child was never in the lead, and what was that child's total after the five spins?

137 | PALINDROMIC

I have assigned to each letter of the alphabet a different number from 0 to 25. Therefore, for example, a three-letter word might stand for a number of three, four, five or six digits. In fact all the letters used in

PALINDROMIC

have even values. Furthermore, the number represented by this word contains no zeros and is indeed palindromic.

Please send in the number represented by PIN.

138 | CRICKETING GREATS

On each of the next seven evenings a different media pundit will advocate the merits of two cricketers. The pundits are Agnew, Blofeld, Dagnall, Mann, Mitchell, Norcross and Smith.

The fourteen cricketers to be discussed are Ali, Anderson, Ball, Ballance, Broad, Carberry, Compton, Hales, Kerrigan, Patel, Stokes, Tredwell, Trescothick and Woakes. Each evening, looking at the names of the pundit and the two cricketers, then for any two out of the three names there are just two letters of the alphabet that occur (once or more) in both.

(a) Which cricketers will Dagnall advocate?
(b) Which cricketers will Norcross advocate?

139 | FOND MEMORIES

One of my memories of my grandparents' house is of an ornament consisting of three monkeys with the caption "See no evil, hear no evil, speak no evil."

I have written down four odd numbers, one of them being the sum of the other three. Then I have consistently replaced digits with letters, using different letters for different digits. In this way the four numbers have become

SPEAK HEAR SEE EVIL

What number is represented by SPEAK?

140 | ALGEBRIA'S STANDARD

The Algebrian rectangular flag is highly symbolic. Each of its sides is an even number of inches long and a diagonal divides it into two triangles, one blue and one green, representing its two founding tribes. The length of the diagonal (in inches) is the number of states in Algebria, and the area of the flag (in square inches) is the 20th-century year in which the country obtained independence.

How many states are there in Algebria, and in which year did the country obtain independence?

141 | LITTLE TIME

Do you have a little time to try this Teaser? I have taken a four-figure number and a six-figure number and I have consistently replaced digits by letters to give the words:

LITTLE and TIME

If you take the digits of TIME and write down all the four-figure numbers which use exactly those digits in some order and then add up all those numbers, then your total will be LITTLE.

What number is TIME?

142 | SEQUENCE OF SQUARES

I started with a rectangle of paper. With one straight cut I divided it into a square and a rectangle. I put the square to one side and started again with the remaining rectangle. With one straight cut I divided it into a square and a rectangle. I put the square (which was smaller than the previous one) to one side and started again with the remaining rectangle. I kept repeating this process (discarding a smaller square each time) until eventually the remaining rectangle was itself a square and it had sides of length one centimetre. So overall I had divided the original piece of paper into squares. The average area of the squares was a two-figure number of square centimetres.

What were the dimensions of the original rectangle?

143 | SEVENTH HEAVEN?

I have a modern painting by the surrealist artist Doolali. It is called "Seventh Heaven" and it consists of a triangle with green sides and a red spot on each of its sides. The red spots are one seventh of the way along each side as you pass clockwise around the triangle. Then each of the red spots is joined by a straight blue line to the opposite corner of the triangle. These three blue lines create a new triangle within the original one and the new triangle has area $100cm^2$.

What is the area of the green triangle?

144 | ON THE RACK

I have wine in a rectangular rack consisting of five rows and eight columns. The bottles are made up of five different vintages with each vintage (four reds and four whites) forming a rectangle in the rack. Within each vintage-rectangle the places occupied by the whites form a connected set, and the same is true of the reds. No two vintage-rectangles have the same red/white pattern, no matter what angle they are viewed at from the front. In the rack the first row is a mixture of reds and whites, with a red on the extreme right. Another row contains just reds, and the first column contains more reds than than any other column.

What (in order) are the colours of the wines in the second row?

145 | CLUMSY MEG

I arranged cards labelled ONE, TWO, THREE, FOUR, FIVE, SIX, SEVEN, EIGHT, NINE and TEN equally-spaced around the perimeter of a circular table. The arrangement was such that any two adjacent cards had exactly one letter in common.

That evening Meg entered the room and accidentally knocked two adjacent cards onto the floor. In her haste to put things right, she inadvertently put the two cards back the wrong way round. Surprisingly, the one-letter property still applied.

What were the two numbers directly opposite the two that she knocked on the floor?

146 | PRIME LOGIC

Three expert logicians played a game with a set of twenty-one cards each containing a different two-figure prime number. Each drew a card and held it up so that they could not see their own card but could see the others. Alf, Bert and Charlie in turn were then asked two questions, namely "Is your number the smallest of the three?" and "Is your number the largest of the three?". In the first round all three answered "Don't know" to both questions. The same happened in rounds two and three. In round four Alf answered "Don't know" to the first question.

What did Alf answer to the second question and what numbers did Bert and Charlie have?

147 | CUBIC SAVINGS

In 2009 George and Martha had a four-figure number of pounds in a special savings account (interest being paid into a separate current account). At the end of the year they decided to give some of it away, the gift being shared equally among their seven grandchildren, with each grandchild getting a whole number of pounds. At the end of the following year they did a similar thing with a different-sized gift, but again each grandchild received an equal whole number of pounds. They have repeated this procedure at the end of every year since.

The surprising thing is that, at all times, the number of pounds in the savings account has been a perfect cube.

What is the largest single gift received by any grandchild?

148 | LUCKY DIP

My bank PIN consists of four different digits in decreasing order. I used this PIN to help me choose my six lottery numbers. I wrote down all the two-figure numbers that used two different digits from the PIN. Just six of those numbers were in the range from 10 to 49 and so they were my lottery choices. In fact the sum of the six is a perfect square. If you knew that square it would now be possible to work out my PIN.

What is my PIN?

149 | FIVE-CARD TRICK

I have five cards with a different digit from 1 to 5 on each. I shuffled them and placed them face-down in a row to form a concealed five-figure number. Then I invited each of my six nephews to choose a number less than fifty and they happened to choose six consecutive numbers. Then I explained that there would be a prize for anyone whose number was a factor of the concealed number. No-one was certain to win but they were all in with a chance until I revealed the final digit of the number, which ruled out two of them from winning. Then I revealed the first digit and that ruled two more out. Then I revealed the whole number and just one nephew won a prize.

What was the concealed number?

150 | APPROPRIATE ARITHMETIC

I wrote down three two-figure numbers, one of which was double one of the others. Overall the three numbers used six consecutive digits between them. I then added up the three numbers to give a three-figure sum, and I also multiplied together the three numbers to give a five-figure product. Replacing digits consistently by letters my two answers, appropriately, were ADD and TIMES.

What were the three original numbers?

151 | CIRCULAR LOGIC

Ten of us (me, Alice, Arnold, Carla, Celia, Clara, Ina, Rona, Ronald and Roland) were sitting equally-spaced around a circular table. None of us was directly opposite or next to anyone whose name was an anagram of theirs, or between two people whose names were anagrams of each other. The same applied when looking at the initial letters of the names. Then Ari and Ira joined us. We found two extra chairs and all budged up to make two spaces. With the twelve of us equally-spaced around the circular table all the above facts remained true. I was now opposite a different person, Roland.

Who from the twelve was then directly opposite Alice? And who was opposite Celia?

152 | AN AGE-OLD PROGRESSION

It is my birthday today – the same day as two of my younger relatives, Betty and Charles. I commented that the digits involved in our three ages are all different. Betty noted that the square of her age is equal to my age multiplied by Charles's age. Then Charles added that on one of our birthdays in the next ten years the sum of our ages will be one hundred.

What are our three ages today?

153 | EASY AS ABC

I have ten cards and on each is one of the letters A, B, C, E, L, N, T, V, W and Y. On the back of each card is a different digit.

The digits on T, E, N add to 10.
The digits on T, W, E, L, V, E add to 12.
The digits on T, W, E, N, T, Y add to 20.
The digits on A, B, C add to ....

If I told you that last total, then you should be able to answer the following question:

What are the digits on T, E and N respectively?

154 | BONFIRE TOFFEE

In this subtraction sum I have consistently replaced digits with letters, different letters being used for different digits:

BONFIRE – TOFFEE = TREATS

Please send in the number of ENTRIES.

155 | FOUR STEADINGS AND A NUMERAL

Farmers Al, Bo, Cy and Di have different double-digit numbers of sheep kept in their respective steadings. Al has the fewest and his number of sheep is a certain fraction of Bo's number of sheep. Also, Bo's number of sheep is that same fraction of Cy's number, and Cy's number is that same fraction of Di's.

If I told you the total of Bo's number of sheep added to Cy's, then you would be unable to work out all their numbers of sheep. Similarly, if instead I told you just Bo's number of sheep, then you would be unable to work out all the other numbers.

What (in the order Al, Bo, Cy, Di) are their numbers of sheep?

156 | MAGIC SLIDES

I have a toy consisting of eight tiles that can move by sliding them around a three-by-three frame:

1	2	3
4	5	6
7	8	

At any stage a tile adjacent to the space can slide into that space. I gave the toy to my grandson in the state illustrated and after some moves he presented it back to me with the space once again in the bottom right-hand corner but with the "2" (among others) not in its original position. Furthermore, his arrangement had some "magical" properties: each row, each column, and the diagonal from bottom left to top right all added up to the same total.

What was his arrangement?

157 | SILLY SLIP

Please help me find my silly slip. I correctly added a five-figure number to a four-figure number to give a six-figure total. Then I tried to substitute letters for digits systematically and I ended up with

$$\text{SILLY} + \text{SLIP} = \text{PLEASE}$$

However, in these letters I have made one silly slip, so please find it and then work out what the correct sum was.

What was the correct six-figure numerical answer?

158 | GOLFING GREATS

Following the success of this summer's programmes about cricketing greats, there is to be an equivalent series about golfers. On each of the next seven evenings a different media pundit will advocate the merits of two golfers. The pundits are Coltart, Critchley, Harmon, Livingstone, Lee, Murray and Roe. The fourteen golfers to be discussed are Chappell, Els, Faldo, Harrington, Hogan, McIlroy, Moore, Nicklaus, Poulter, Reed, Singh, Snead, Stenson, and Woods. Each evening, looking at the names of the pundit and the two golfers, then for any two out of the three names there are just two letters of the alphabet that occur (once or more) in both.

(a) Which golfers will Critchley advocate?
(b) Which golfers will Harmon advocate?

159 | A MONTH OF MEETINGS

In one particular month this year I had one-day meetings in each of Geneva, London, Rome, Tallin, Venice and York. For any two of these cities their names had at least one letter in common precisely when the days of their meetings (1st, 2nd, 3rd ...) had no common factor larger than one. No two meetings were on the same day of the week (eg, no two meetings were on Wednesdays). The Geneva meeting was the first and the London meeting was the last, the London meeting being on a Friday.

What was the date of the Tallin meeting (month and day)?

160 | SNOW WHITE

Snow White placed three balls in a hat ("Oh yes she did!"): written on each ball was a different non-zero digit. She asked one of her little helpers to draw out the three in some order and to use them in that order to make a three-figure number. She knew that this number would be divisible by three but not by seven. She asked the helpers to share out that number of sweets equally among the seven of them as far as possible and to give her the remainder. On seeing the remaining sweets she was always able to work out the order in which the three digits had been drawn out.

What (in increasing order) were the three digits?

161 | HAPPY XMAS

I wrote down three perfect squares. In each square precisely three of its digits were even, the rest being odd. Then I consistently replaced digits by letters, with different letters for different digits. In this way the three squares became appropriately

HAPPY XMAS TIMES

What number does TIMES represent?

162 | FAREWELL

Today I am retiring after editing this column for 40 very pleasurable years. My heartfelt thanks go out to all the setters and solvers of puzzles with whom I have corresponded.

To celebrate the 40 years I threw a party for the puzzle-setters. At the party we assigned a different whole number from 1 to 26 to each letter of the alphabet; for example, we had A=13 and Z=3. We did this in such a way that, for each person present (including me), the values of the letters of their Christian name added to 40. Bob, Graham, Hugh, Nick and Richard were there, as were two of Andrew, Angela, Danny, Des, Ian, John, Mike, Peter, Robin, Steve and Tom.

Which two?

163 | CROQUET MALLET

My croquet mallet is less than a metre high and consists of a cylindrical shaft attached to a heavier cuboid head, both of uniform density. Knowing the total weight of the mallet, I wanted to work out the weight of the shaft. I found the point of balance along the shaft and measured the distances from there to each end of the shaft, the smaller of which was less than the height of the head. Each of these three distances was a whole prime number of cm, and taking the three distances together with the height of the mallet, no digit was repeated.

I worked out that the weight of the head was a single digit multiple of the weight of the shaft.

What was the height of my mallet?

164 | METAL ARITHMETIC

The area of one face of a hot, steel cuboid block was a single-figure whole number of square feet; and it was within one per cent of this after cooling and contraction. When cool, it was cut, parallel to this face, into blocks of the same width and height, but unequal length. For the first cut block, its width, height and length, in inches, were different two-figure whole numbers with only four factors (including 1 and the number), and they had only the factor 1 in common. The same applied to the other cut blocks. Curiously, the six digits of the width, height and length of the first cut block were also all different.

In ascending order, what were the dimensions, in inches, of the shortest block?

165 | A CONVIVIAL DINNER PARTY

Three married couples, the Blacks, the Grays and the Pinks, are having dinner together seated around a circular table. The three men had provided one course each towards the dinner. Each lady was sitting between two men, neither being her husband. The first names are Henry, Robin, Tom, Jenny, Monica and Naomi. Robin and Mr Pink go to the same gym as the wife of the provider of the starter and Mrs Gray. The main course provider, an only child, has Monica on his right. The starter provider doesn't have a sister. The dessert came from someone sitting closer to Naomi than he is to Mrs Black. Henry is brother in law to the starter provider and his only sister is on his left. Tom's wife made the coffee, whilst the other two ladies washed up.

What were the full names of all the ladies?

166 | TWO SUMS

Digits have been systematically replaced by letters to give:

ONE + ONE = TWO
ONE + FOUR = FIVE

No number consists of a consecutive set of digits.

What number is represented by FIFTEEN?

167 | CATCHING THE BUS

I can travel to town by either the number 12 bus or the number 15 bus. The number 12 bus leaves every 12 minutes and the number 15 bus leaves every 15 minutes.

The first number 15 bus leaves soon after the first number 12 bus. I arrive at the bus stop at random and catch the first bus to arrive.

If the probability of me catching the number 15 bus is 2/5 how soon does the first number 15 bus leave after the first number 12 bus?

168 | SQUARES ON CUBES

Liam has a set of ten wooden cubes; each has a different number (from 1 to 10) painted on one face (the other five faces are blank). He has arranged them in a rectangular block with all numbers upright and facing outwards. Each vertical side of the block shows some numbers which can be read as a perfect square. No two squares have the same number of digits.

Which square must be present?

169 | NINE CUT DIAMONDS

An app "shuffles" and "deals" the "ace" (=1) to "nine" of diamonds in a line, face down. Three numbers under 30 are chosen at random and each will win if it is a factor of the hidden nine-digit value. Keying # reveals the rightmost face-down card. At such a "reveal" the app displays "won", "lost" or "in-play" for each number. The rightmost face-down cards are revealed singly until all are known. For one deal my three numbers didn't include a prime number and after two "reveals" were all "in-play". After the third "reveal", two were "won" and one "lost".

At the third "reveal" what three-digit number was displayed?

170 | POLITICAL PAIRINGS

A debating society arranged for a series of eight political debates between different Labour and Conservative politicians, each time with a different presenter. The presenters were: MARR, NEIL, NEWMAN, PARKINSON, PAXMAN, POPPLEWELL, ROBINSON and SNOW. The Labour politicians were: ABBOTT, ABRAHAMS, CHAKRABARTI, CORBYN, EAGLE, LEWIS, STARMER and WATSON. The Conservative politicians were: BRADLEY, GRAYLING, GREEN, HAMMOND, LEADSOM, LIDINGTON, MCLOUGHLIN and MUNDELL. For each debate there were 2 letters in common for any pairing from presenter, Labour politician and Conservative politician. The Labour politicians are listed alphabetically.

What is the corresponding order for the Conservative politicians?

171 | WIN SOME, LOSE SOME

The six teams in our local league play each other once in the season. Last season no two teams tied on points. Here is part of the table from the end of that season, with the teams in alphabetical order. However, digits have been consistently replaced by letters.

	Played	Won	Lost	Drawn	Goals for	Goals against	Points
Albion	W	O	N				
Borough		S	O	M	E		
City			L	O	S	T	
Friday				S	O	M	E

Please send in the number of LEMONS.

172 | TIME DUALITY

After a good breakfast, Seb decided on 40 winks. He noted the time on his digital clock as he dozed off. When he woke up a little later that day, not fully alert, he saw the display reflected in a mirror and was amazed by how long he seemed to have slept. This was in fact ten times the length of his nap. Next day, a similar thing happened: he fell asleep at the same time and slept a little less, but when he woke, the mirror led him to believe he had slept for 20 times as long as he had. (All times were whole numbers of minutes after midnight.)

At what time did he fall asleep?

173 | SPANISH AND LATIN

I have ten cards. For each card there is a number in Spanish on one side and a number in Latin on the other. The Spanish numbers are CINCO, CUATRO, DIEZ, DOS, NUEVE, OCHO, SEIS, SIETE, TRES and UNO. The Latin numbers are DECEM, DUO, NOVEM, OCTO, QUATTUOR, QUINQUE, SEPTEM, SEX, TRES and UNUS. For each of the ten pairs of numbers, there are two letters in common. If I told you on how many cards the two numbers were consecutive, you should be able to work out all ten pairings. The Spanish numbers are written alphabetically.

What is the corresponding order for the Latin numbers?

174 | LIGHT ANGLES

The hotel's night clerk was always glancing at the novelty 12-hour clock facing her. Its hands' rotation axis was exactly midway across and between three-quarters and four-fifths of the way up the four-metre high rectangular wall. Light rays directed out along the continuous-motion minute and hour hands made pencil beams across the wall. Twice during her 12-hour shift she saw the beams hit the top corners of the wall simultaneously, and twice she saw the beams hit the bottom corners simultaneously.

How wide was the wall to the nearest metre?

175 | EASTER EGG

"Granddad, I've got a great big Easter egg in a square box!". My grandson Liam inspired this Teaser in which I have used non-zero digits then consistently replaced them with letters, using different letters for different digits.

In this way, I have

$$\text{EASTER} \; (\text{EGG})^2 \; \text{BOX}$$

Two of the numbers add to make the third, and if I told you which number was largest you should be able to solve this Teaser.

Send in your BOX.

176 | MY VALENTINE

Using only positive digits, MILLY wrote down a two-digit number and a nine-digit number, both numbers being divisible by 14.

Splitting her nine-digit number into three three-digit numbers, she noticed that all three numbers were also divisible by 14.

Systematically replacing different digits by different letters, her two-digit number and nine-digit number ended up as MY VALENTINE.

What number is represented by MILLY?

177 | BASE JUMPING

In written multiplication tests Jay always calculated correct answers, but, quirkily, wrote the digits of any two-figure answers in reverse order. A completed test sheet (pre-printed with ordered triplets of single-figure positive integers to multiply, eg, 1x2x2= and 3x5x9=) included a question and his two-figure written answer that would be right when thought of in a number base other than 'base 10' (any numerals keeping their usual values). Jay told Kay about this, but didn't give the question or answer. Kay asked whether one of that question's numbers to multiply was a particular value and from the reply knew both the question and the answer Jay had written.

What was Jay's written answer to that question?

178 | AN ANCESTRAL EQUATION

I recently discovered a 16th-century ancestor called David, which happens to be my maiden name. (I never really liked Bricket, even when pronounced in the French way.) I have always been partial to word arithmetic (or cryptarithms) and the other day I found a solution to this one:

$$MY \times NAME = DAVID$$

When eight distinct digits are substituted for the eight letters and no number starts with zero, the equation holds. Amazingly the solution gave me more information about my ancestor. MY turned out to be his age when he died and NAME was the year he was born.

What was that year?

179 | SQUARE DEAL

George and Martha have five daughters who have periodically appeared in my teasers over the years. They are all working for the same company and have perfect-square four-digit telephone extensions, in all five cases. The letters ABCDEFGHIJ stand for the digits 0-9 but in no particular order. The extensions are as follows:

Andrea	IBHC
Bertha	DJJC
Caroline	BAFH
Dorothy	GFID
Elizabeth	GAEE

What are the five extensions?

180 | BIRTHDAYS 2018

Several friends have birthdays on different days in 2018.

Replacing A by 1, B by 2, C by 3 … and Z by 26, each month and day can be replaced by a sequence of numbers. Every birthday is given numerically by day, date and month, as described above. For each friend, there is just one number common to each of their three sets of numbers. The number of friends is the largest possible.

How many friends are there and what is the largest number of clear days between consecutive birthdays?

181 | WHAT'S MY CARD?

Four expert logicians play a game with a pack of six cards, numbered from 1 to 6. The cards are shuffled and each draws a card, holding it in front of him so that he cannot see his own number but can see the numbers held by the others. The winner is the player who can first deduce what number he is holding. Each player in turn is asked to announce the sum of two numbers that he can see on the other cards. One game started with Alf announcing 6. After a long pause, no-one claimed victory, so Bert then announced 5. There was a significant pause, but before Charlie spoke, someone claimed victory.

Which cards did Alf and Bert hold, and which cards remained on the table?

182 | CATCHING ANOTHER BUS

I want to catch a bus into town, and I arrive at the bus stop at a random time.

The number 12 bus runs every 12 minutes, the number 15 bus runs every 15 minutes and the number 20 bus runs every 20 minutes.

All the buses leave the bus stop at an exact number of minutes past the hour and no two buses leave at the same time.

Interestingly, given the above information, the probability that I catch a number 12 bus is as small as it possibly could be.

What is the probability that I catch a number 12 bus?

183 | TRACKWORD

George and Martha are tackling a Trackword problem which appears in magazines. Nine letters are placed in a three-by-three grid and you have to work from one square to a neighbour, proceeding up, down, left, right or diagonally until all nine squares have been visited to form a nine-letter word. You must start in the top-left corner. As an example, you can get the word EIGHTFOLD from the following grid:

E	T	H
F	I	G
O	L	D

George and Martha thought that would be interesting to work out how many possible routes there are which start in the top-left corner.

How many routes are there?

184 | IN PROPORTION

In 2000 the Sultan of Proportion told his five sons they would inherit his fortune in amounts proportionate to their ages at his death.

Accordingly, they each recently received a different whole number of tesares. Strangely, if he had lived a few more hours the five ages would have been consecutive and each son would again have received a whole number of tesares. Such a delay would have benefited just one son (by 1000 tesares).

How many tesares were distributed in total?

185 | COMBINATORIAL CARDS

On holiday once with lost luggage and trapped indoors, we decided to recreate our favourite card game. With limited resources, we used just seven cards and seven images (red heart, green tree etc) with three images on each card. Remarkably, just as in the game at home, every pair of cards had exactly one image in common. Labelling the seven images from 1 to 7, the cards were as follows:

$$\{1,2,4\}\ \{2,3,6\}\ \{1,3,5\}\ \{1,6,7\}$$
$$\{2,5,7\}\ \{3,4,7\}\ \{4,5,6\}$$

Interestingly, each image appears on just three cards.

Our original set of cards at home has eight images per card, each image appears on just eight cards and again the total number of images is the same as the number of cards.

What is that number?

186 | NUMBER CHALLENGE

I challenged Charlotte and Oliver to find a nine-digit number, using nine different digits, so that

- The number given by the 1st and 2nd digits was divisible by 2.
- The number given by the 2nd and 3rd digits was divisible by 3.

And so on until

- The number given by the 8th and 9th digits was divisible by 9.

They each produced a different, correct solution. Charlotte claimed hers was the better solution since in her number, the number formed by the first seven digits was also divisible by 7, Charlotte's age.

What was Charlotte's number?

187 | PENSIONABLE SERVICE

A few years ago my father was lucky enough to have been able to retire and take his pension at sixty. I explained to my young son – not yet a teenager – that this was not now usual, and that neither I nor he would be so lucky in the future.

When I am as old as my father is now, I shall be six times my son's present age. By then, my son will be nine years older than I am now. (These statements all refer to whole years and not fractions of years.)

How old am I now?

188 | LIVING ON THE COAST

George and Martha are living on Pythag Island. Not surprisingly, it is in the shape of a right-angled triangle, and each side is an integral number of miles (under one hundred) long. Martha noticed that the area of the island (expressed in square miles) was equal to an exact multiple of its perimeter (expressed in miles). George was trying to work out that multiple, but gave up: "Please write down the appropriate digit." he said. "Impossible!" said Martha.

What are the lengths of the coasts?

189 | REMEMBERING PINS

My 10-year-old grandson has several PINs of various lengths to remember.

To help him in this, he has systematically replaced different digits by different letters to get corresponding words as THREE, FIVE, SIX, SEVEN, NINE, TEN and FIFTEEN. Being very clever, he has arranged it so that each PIN is divisible by the number specified by the corresponding word.

What is his PIN for FIFTEEN?

190 | BE CRAFTY AND BOX CLEVER

Tyson, a crafter, had several cylindrical enclosed boxes (with heights equal to diameters) in two sizes. Each box's surface area (including top and bottom) was a three-figure integer in square centimetres, and the larger boxes had a radius which was a whole number multiple of that of the smaller boxes.

He kept them all in one vertical stack, to within one centimetre of the top of their metre-deep storage bin. Whilst working out fabric-cutting schemes, Tyson found that all the bigger boxes' surface areas combined equalled all the smaller boxes' surface areas combined and that the total surface area (in square centimetres) of all the boxes had all its numerals in ascending order.

What was the total surface area of all the boxes, in square centimetres?

191 | RETURN TICKETS

In our tombola the tickets were numbered consecutively from 1 upwards and were printed in books of 20. A local airline donated the prizes – a number of tickets to Paris and back. We decided to split the prizes into single-journey tickets and award them in an unusual way. If any ticket number had all different digits which were in increasing order then it won an outward flight to Paris: if it had all different digits which were in decreasing order then it won a flight back from Paris. So, for example, number 145 won an outward flight, number 30 won a flight back, and single-figure numbers were lucky enough to win tickets there and back. Luckily we had exactly the right number of tickets for all the prizes to be awarded.

How many tickets did we print?

192 | BANK STATEMENT

My last bank statement was most interesting. The first line showed the opening balance in pounds and pence, then each of the following four lines showed a debit together with the resulting balance. I did not go overdrawn.

Remarkably, each of the five balances used the same five different digits once only, and the largest of the digits was less than three times the smallest. Each of the four debits also used five different digits once only, but the digits in the debits were all different from those in the balances.

What was the final balance?

193 | £SD

50 years ago, the coins in circulation were the halfpenny (1/2d), penny (1d), threepenny bit (3d), sixpence (6d), shilling (12d), florin (2 shillings) and half crown (2 shillings and sixpence).

One day, having at least one of each of the above coins, I decided to bank them.

The cashier set out the coins in separate piles, checked them (discovering that the number of coins in each pile was a square), and gave me exactly a 10-shilling note in exchange.

If I told you how many different numbers of coins were in those piles, you should be able to work out the numbers of each coin.

In the order half crown down to halfpenny, how many coins of each type were there?

194 | POINTLESS BATTING AVERAGES

When my son was chosen to play cricket for his School First XI, I kept a record of the number of runs he scored in each of his first five innings. After each innings I calculated his batting average (the total number of runs scored so far divided by the number of innings) and found an interesting pattern:

(i) Each score was under 30
(ii) They were all different
(iii) Each of the five averages was a whole number

When he asked me how he could maintain this pattern with his sixth innings, I was able to tell him the smallest score that would achieve this.

What is the largest number this could have been?

195 | POLYGOLAND

We've all heard of Heligoland but George and Martha are on holiday in Polygoland. This is an island and when it was first inhabited, the authorities created as many national parks as possible subject to the restriction that each such park will be a regular polygon with the angle between each side being an integral number of degrees, and all the parks have different numbers of sides. Walking along the border between two such parks, Martha commented that the angle (A) of one of them was an exact multiple of the number of sides (S) in the other. George mentioned that the multiple was equal to the number of parks on the island.

What are A and S?

196 | PRIME MULTIPLICATION

Almost everyone knows that the single digit prime numbers are 2, 3, 5, and 7, the number 1 having been excluded quite a long time ago. Here is a multiplication involving prime digits:

```
      p p p
    x   p p
    -------
    p p p p
  p p p p
  ---------
  p p p p p
  ---------
```

What is the answer?

197 | LETTERS PUZZLE

My best friend has a special birthday later this month, and I have composed a Teaser to celebrate the occasion. First of all, I wrote that date as a single number (with the day at the start, the month in the middle and the year at the end).

Then, replacing different letters consistently with different non-zero digits, I found that the sum of LETTERS and PUZZLE gives that number.

Send in your prime value for TEASER.

198 | BARCODE

When Fred opened his "10 to 99 Store" (the numbers reflecting the prices of the goods in pounds) there was trouble from the start when the barcode reader scanned the prices backwards. First at the self-service checkout was Mrs Adams, who kept quiet when she was charged £59.49 for a £94.95 item. The next two customers, Mr Baker and Mr Coles, paid by card, without noticing they had in fact been overcharged. All three had bought a differently-priced item, and by coincidence, in the case of the two men, the price each had been charged was a whole multiple of the actual price.

How much had the shop lost or gained overall on the three transactions?

199 | OCTAVIA THE OCTAGONARIAN

Queen Octavia's emblem was two concentric regular octagons (the outermost's side length equal to the innermost's distance between opposite sides). Seen from above her eightieth-birthday, level, cheesecake torte, with octagonal cavity all the way through and vertical side-faces, matched the emblem. Its outer side-faces were square and a two-figure whole number of inches wide. A four-feet diameter cylindrical cover protected it. At the party the whole torte was used, without wastage, to levelly fill a number of identical cuboid dishes (internally having length, width and depth, in inches, each a different single-figure whole number greater than one). Curiously, the number of dishes was a three-figure value with different numerals in descending order.

What was the torte's volume in cubic inches?

200 | INSCRIBED

The Republic of Mathematica has an unusual rectangular flag. It measures 120cm by 60cm and has a red background. It features a green triangle and a white circle. All the lengths of the sides of the triangle and the radius of the circle (which touches all three sides of the triangle) are whole numbers of cm. Also, the distances from the vertices of the triangle to the centre of the circle are whole numbers of cm. The flag has a line of symmetry.

What is the length of the shortest side of the triangle?

SOLUTIONS

TEASER 1
1, 6, 7 and 8

TEASER 2
1, 3, 3 and 3

TEASER 3
(a) 3-1 and 1-0 (b) 2-0 and 0-1

TEASER 4
1098

TEASER 5
SEND = 3568

TEASER 6
19 and 103

TEASER 7
1, 3, 7 and 9

TEASER 8
7 square metres

TEASER 9
1!, 8! and 9!

TEASER 10
13, 21, 23, 24, 41, 43

TEASER 11
2 hours

TEASER 12
80429

TEASER 13
5th April and 27th December

TEASER 14
49, 576, 1089 and 3025

TEASER 15
Sue 14, Terry 98

TEASER 16
121 miles

TEASER 17
November 29th

TEASER 18
1, 3, 4, 5, 6 and 8

TEASER 19
286

TEASER 20
961178

TEASER 21
157, 283 and 409

TEASER 22
2197

TEASER 23
Derry House; 12, 6, 5 and 3

TEASER 24
50 square metres

TEASER 25
45 red and 342 blue

TEASER 26
William, Samuel, Robert, Newman and Michael

TEASER 27
6006 metres

TEASER 28
26/05/1936

TEASER 29
8

TEASER 30
(a) 15:43, 26/07/89 (b) 18:59, 27/06/34

TEASER 31
27cm and 54cm

TEASER 32
2/5/40

TEASER 33
24

TEASER 34
Twelve and fifteen

TEASER 35
Shahzad, Robson, Carberry, Tredwell, Compton, Stokes

TEASER 36
1, 3 and 6

TEASER 37
Lear 5; Cordelia 1, 2 and 6

TEASER 38
60 metres by 169 metres

TEASER 39
854

TEASER 40
9 faces, 8 of which were triangular

TEASER 41
(a) 4 (b) 2 (c) 4

TEASER 42
3, 6, 9, 17 and 19

TEASER 43
LLLLWDW

TEASER 44
2074

TEASER 45
40cm

TEASER 46
10 balls, 4 of which were red

TEASER 47
54 miles

TEASER 48
Lampard, Suarez, Aguero, Neymar, Ibrahimovic and Schweinsteiger

TEASER 49
69357

TEASER 50
6006

TEASER 51
Daughter; 1, 2, 5, 9, 10 King; 16

TEASER 52
7/12

TEASER 53
Doris, Natasha and Lana

TEASER 54
February, July and December

TEASER 55
324 and 784

TEASER 56
95 people, including 9 vegetarians

TEASER 57
6

TEASER 58
(a) October; (b) R and Y

TEASER 59
3901

TEASER 60
4 metres

TEASER 61
752 and 346

TEASER 62
5

TEASER 63
£15, £14 and £8

TEASER 64
18, 15, 9, 7 and 3

TEASER 65
H, K, D, B, L, I, H, R, J, F, H, S

TEASER 66
June 27th

TEASER 67
£16, £12 and £9

TEASER 68
6, 7, 8 and 9

TEASER 69
4, 8, 11 and 13

TEASER 70
SUNDAY = 816270

TEASER 71

54

TEASER 72

101123595

TEASER 73

10, 11, 14 and 15

TEASER 74

932801

TEASER 75

3842

TEASER 76

64 and 91

TEASER 77

176 miles

TEASER 78

Clarke, Allen, Thompson, Croker, McLean, McGilchrist

TEASER 79

11 teams; Villa 1 — Wanderers 0

TEASER 80

8, 9, 16, 27, 30 and 45

TEASER 81

5, 2, 3, 6, 7, 1, 9, 0, 8, 4

TEASER 82

4 2 0 1 5 3

TEASER 83

7 red and 15 black

TEASER 84

12cm by 21cm

TEASER 85
61 cm^2

TEASER 86
3155

TEASER 87
2123

TEASER 88
11 02 24 and 07 02 25

TEASER 89
257

TEASER 90
738

TEASER 91
£3.20

TEASER 92
127026

TEASER 93
2592

TEASER 94
Blunt, Carter, Margolyes, Arterton, Knightley, Jones and Watson

TEASER 95
(a) 76; (b) Vic

TEASER 96
12876435

TEASER 97
Colin, 20

TEASER 98
8778

TEASER 99

3, 7, 9 and 13

TEASER 100

38

TEASER 101

1006

TEASER 102

4371

TEASER 103

The sum of Wunce's squares was 1989; the sum of Repete's squares was 831.

TEASER 104

CBA 777 F

TEASER 105

9721

TEASER 106

324 576 1089

TEASER 107

3211278

TEASER 108

01 48 59 27

TEASER 107

8, 1, 4, 6, 3, 7, 9, 2 and 5

TEASER 110

August 5th, 12th, 26th and 27th

TEASER 111

J, P, H, C, J, H, S, R, C, S, R, P

TEASER 112

41 and 961

TEASER 113
8

TEASER 114
30, 42, 60 and 72cm

TEASER 115
1001 and 0110

TEASER 116
1, 2, 4, 4, 6, 7

TEASER 117
largest = 50; product = 251

TEASER 118
49 and 64

TEASER 119
410

TEASER 120
384912

TEASER 121
987362411112

TEASER 122
3/140

TEASER 123
0-0, 0-1, 2-0, 1-0, 0-3, 0-0

TEASER 124
4, 4, 5, 5 and 6

TEASER 125
439351

TEASER 126
1

TEASER 127
42 inches and 30 inches

TEASER 128
1 and 9

TEASER 129
25

TEASER 130
CCXVI and LXXIX

TEASER 131
24, 36 and 70

TEASER 132
147456

TEASER 133
57209

TEASER 134
11cm

TEASER 135
50 and 75

TEASER 136
Nancy, 15

TEASER 137
24412

TEASER 138
(a) Ball and Broad (b) Ballance and Woakes

TEASER 139
12507

TEASER 140
68 and 1920

TEASER 141

3578

TEASER 142

13cm by 21cm

TEASER 143

172cm^2

TEASER 144

R W W W W W W R

TEASER 145

7 and 8

TEASER 146

"No", 47 and 59

TEASER 147

£388

TEASER 148

5420

TEASER 149

15324

TEASER 150

23, 46 and 75

TEASER 151

Rona and Ira

TEASER 152

63, 21 and 7

TEASER 153

3, 2 and 5

TEASER 154

9276390

TEASER 155
16, 24, 36 and 54

TEASER 156
237 615 48

TEASER 157
106496

TEASER 158
(a) Moore and Reed (b) Singh and Snead

TEASER 159
March 22nd

TEASER 160
4, 8 and 9

TEASER 161
31684

TEASER 162
Des and Mike

TEASER 163
90cm

TEASER 164
21, 34 and 55in

TEASER 165
Monica Pink, Naomi Gray, Jenny Black

TEASER 166
9594663

TEASER 167
1.5 minutes

TEASER 168
9

TEASER 169

528

TEASER 170

LEADSOM, GRAYLING, HAMMOND, LIDINGTON, GREEN, BRADLEY, MUNDELL, MCLOUGHLIN

TEASER 171

LEMONS = 370124

TEASER 172

09:41am

TEASER 173

NOVEM, TRES, DECEM, DUO, UNUS, OCTO, SEPTEM, QUINQUE, SEX and QUATTUOR

TEASER 174

16m

TEASER 175

362

TEASER 176

17224

TEASER 177

48

TEASER 178

1543

TEASER 179

2916, 5776, 9801, 3025 and 3844

TEASER 180

4 and 81

TEASER 181

Alf 3, Bert 5, with 2 and 6 on the table

TEASER 182
7/20
TEASER 183
138
TEASER 184
383160
TEASER 185
57
TEASER 186
187254963
TEASER 187
34
TEASER 188
65, 72 and 97
TEASER 189
1412550
TEASER 190
3456 sq. cm.
TEASER 191
1480
TEASER 192
£347.58
TEASER 193
1, 1, 1, 4, 1, 9 and 36
TEASER 194
23
TEASER 195
A = 176, S = 8

TEASER 196

25575

TEASER 197

314719

TEASER 198

The shop had gained £117

TEASER 199

23328 cu. in.

TEASER 200

56 cm

PUZZLE SETTERS

TEASER 1
H Bradley and C Higgins

TEASER 2
Michael Fletcher

TEASER 3
Nick MacKinnon

TEASER 4
Ian Kay

TEASER 5
Andrew Skidmore

TEASER 6
Victor Bryant

TEASER 7
David Buontempo

TEASER 8
Ian Kay

TEASER 9
Nick MacKinnon

TEASER 10
Robin Nayler

TEASER 11
Michael Fletcher

TEASER 12
Graham Smithers

TEASER 13
Victor Bryant

TEASER 14
Andrew Skidmore

TEASER 15
Ian Kay

TEASER 16
Alan Bergson

TEASER 17
H Bradley and C Higgins

TEASER 18
Michael Fletcher

TEASER 19
Victor Bryant

TEASER 20
Andrew Skidmore

TEASER 21
David Buontempo

TEASER 22
Nick MacKinnon

TEASER 23
Angela Newing

TEASER 24
Des MacHale

TEASER 25
Michael Fletcher

TEASER 26
Graham Smithers

TEASER 27
Robin Nayler

TEASER 28
Graham Smithers

TEASER 29
Andrew Skidmore

TEASER 30
Nick MacKinnon

TEASER 31
H Bradley & C Higgins

TEASER 32
Danny Roth

TEASER 33
Michael Fletcher

TEASER 34
Victor Bryant

TEASER 35
Graham Smithers

TEASER 36
Angela Newing

TEASER 37
Nick MacKinnon

TEASER 38
Andrew Skidmore

TEASER 39
Danny Roth

TEASER 40
Michael Fletcher

TEASER 41
Graham Smithers

TEASER 42
Victor Bryant

TEASER 43
John Owen

TEASER 44
Graham Smithers

TEASER 45
Nick MacKinnon

TEASER 46
Richard England

TEASER 47
Danny Roth

TEASER 48
Graham Smithers

TEASER 49
Andrew Skidmore

TEASER 50
Victor Bryant

TEASER 51
Nick MacKinnon

TEASER 52
Ian Kay

TEASER 53
Angela Newing

TEASER 54
Graham Smithers

TEASER 55
Richard England

TEASER 56
Susan Bricket

TEASER 57
Nick MacKinnon

TEASER 58
Victor Bryant

TEASER 59
Susan Bricket

TEASER 60
Graham Smithers

TEASER 61
Danny Roth

TEASER 62
Ian Kay

TEASER 63
Richard England

TEASER 64
Victor Bryant

TEASER 65
Graham Smithers

TEASER 66
Nick MacKinnon

TEASER 67
Richard England

TEASER 68
Tom Wills-Sandford

TEASER 69
Susan Bricket

TEASER 70
Alan Bergson

TEASER 71
Victor Bryant

TEASER 72
Graham Smithers

TEASER 73
Nick MacKinnon

TEASER 74
Andrew Skidmore

TEASER 75
Susan Bricket

TEASER 76
Robin Nayler

TEASER 77
H. Bradley & C. Higgins

TEASER 78
Graham Smithers

TEASER 79
Victor Bryant

TEASER 80
Nick MacKinnon

TEASER 81
Danny Roth

TEASER 82
Angela Newing

TEASER 83
Michael Fletcher

TEASER 84
Des MacHale

TEASER 85
Nick MacKinnon

TEASER 86
Danny Roth

TEASER 87
Victor Bryant

TEASER 88
Richard England

TEASER 89
Graham Smithers

TEASER 90
Bob Walker

TEASER 91
Michael Fletcher

TEASER 92
Andrew Skidmore

TEASER 93
Nick MacKinnon

TEASER 94
Graham Smithers

TEASER 95
Victor Bryant

TEASER 96
Danny Roth

TEASER 97
Angela Newing

TEASER 98
Andrew Skidmore

TEASER 99
Bob Walker

TEASER 100
Michael Fletcher

TEASER 101
John Owen

TEASER 102
Danny Roth

TEASER 103
Victor Bryant

TEASER 104
Stephen Hogg

TEASER 105
Graham Smithers

TEASER 106
Nick MacKinnon

TEASER 107
Andrews Skidmore

TEASER 108
Danny Roth

TEASER 109
Victor Bryant

TEASER 110
Victor Bryant

TEASER 111
Graham Smithers

TEASER 112
Stephen Hogg

TEASER 113
Andrew Skidmore

TEASER 114
Tom Wills-Sandford

TEASER 115
Danny Roth

TEASER 116
Nick MacKinnon

TEASER 117
Mike Fletcher

TEASER 118
Victor Bryant

TEASER 119
Stephen Hogg

TEASER 120
Danny Roth

TEASER 121
Andrew Skidmore

TEASER 122
Stephen Hogg

TEASER 123
Nick MacKinnon

TEASER 124
Mike Fletcher

TEASER 125
Andrew Skidmore

TEASER 126
Victor Bryant

TEASER 127
Stephen Hogg

TEASER 128
Des MacHale

TEASER 129
RBJT Allenby

TEASER 130
Nick MacKinnon

TEASER 131
Mike Fletcher

TEASER 132
Andrew Skidmore

TEASER 133
Victor Bryant

TEASER 134
Stephen Hogg

TEASER 135
Danny Roth

TEASER 136
Angela Newing

TEASER 137
Victor Bryant

TEASER 138
Graham Smithers

TEASER 139
Andrew Skidmore

TEASER 140
Stephen Hogg

TEASER 141
Graham Smithers

TEASER 142
Victor Bryant

TEASER 143
RBJT Allenby

TEASER 144
Nick MacKinnon

TEASER 145
Graham Smithers

TEASER 146
John Owen

TEASER 147
Danny Roth

TEASER 148
Andrew Skidmore

TEASER 149
Stephen Hogg

TEASER 150
Victor Bryant

TEASER 151
Ian Gilchrist

TEASER 152
Angela Newing

TEASER 153
Graham Smithers

TEASER 154
Andrew Skidmore

TEASER 155
Stephen Hogg

TEASER 156
Victor Bryant

TEASER 157
Victor Bryant

TEASER 158
Graham Smithers

TEASER 159
Bernardo Recaman

TEASER 160
Victor Bryant

TEASER 161
Graham Smithers

TEASER 162
Victor Bryant

TEASER 163
John Owen

TEASER 164
Stephen Hogg

TEASER 165
Angela Newing

TEASER 166
Graham Smithers

TEASER 167
Michael Fletcher

TEASER 168
Andrew Skidmore

TEASER 169
Stephen Hogg

TEASER 170
Graham Smithers

TEASER 171
Victor Bryant

TEASER 172
Peter Good

TEASER 173
Graham Smithers

TEASER 174
Stephen Hogg

TEASER 175
Andrew Skidmore

TEASER 176
Graham Smithers

TEASER 177
Stephen Hogg

TEASER 178
Susan Bricket

TEASER 179
Danny Roth

TEASER 180
Graham Smithers

TEASER 181
John Owen

TEASER 182
Michael Fletcher

TEASER 183
Danny Roth

TEASER 184
Andrew Skidmore

TEASER 185
Susan Bricket

TEASER 186
Graham Smithers

TEASER 187
Angela Newing

TEASER 188
Danny Roth

TEASER 189
Graham Smithers

TEASER 190
Stephen Hogg

TEASER 191
Victor Bryant

TEASER 192
John Owen

TEASER 193
Graham Smithers

TEASER 194
Susan Bricket

TEASER 195
Danny Roth

TEASER 196
Angela Newing

TEASER 197
Andrew Skidmore

TEASER 198
Ian Gilchrist

TEASER 199
Stephen Hogg

TEASER 200
Andrew Skidmore